DATE DUE

Culture and Customs of Japan

**Recent title in
Culture and Customs of Asia**

Culture and Customs of Taiwan
Gary Marvin Davison and Barbara E. Reed

Culture and Customs of Japan

Noriko Kamachi

Culture and Customs of Asia
Hanchao Lu, Series Editor

GREENWOOD PRESS
Westport, Connecticut · London

Library of Congress Cataloging-in-Publication Data

Kamachi, Noriko.
    Culture and customs of Japan / Noriko Kamachi.
        p.   cm. — (Culture and customs of Asia, ISSN 1097–0738)
    Includes bibliographical references and index.
    ISBN 0–313–30197–2 (alk. paper)
    1. Japan—Civilization.   I. Title.   II. Series.
DS821.K2357   1999
952—dc21   99–13707

British Library Cataloguing in Publication Data is available.

Library of Congress Catalog Card Number: 99–13707
ISBN: 0–313–30197–2
ISSN: 1097–0738

First published in 1999

Greenwood Press, 88 Post Road West, Westport, CT 06881
An imprint of Greenwood Publishing Group, Inc.
www.greenwood.com

Printed in the United States of America

The paper used in this book complies with the
Permanent Paper Standard issued by the National
Information Standards Organization (Z39.48–1984).

10 9 8 7 6 5 4 3 2 1

To the memory of my mother

Contents

Illustrations

Series Foreword

Geographically, Asia encompasses the vast area from Suez, the Bosporus, and the Ural Mountains eastward to the Bering Sea and from this line southward to the Indonesian archipelago, an expanse that covers about 30 percent of our earth. Conventionally, and especially insofar as culture and customs are concerned, Asia refers primarily to the region east of Iran and south of Russia. This area can be divided in turn into subregions commonly known as South, Southeast, and East Asia, which are the main focus of this series.

The United States has vast interests in this region. In the twentieth century the United States fought three major wars in Asia (namely, the Pacific War of 1941–45, the Korean War of 1950–53, and the Vietnam War of 1965–75), and each had profound impact on life and politics in America. Today, America's major trading partners are in Asia, and in the foreseeable future the weight of Asia in American life will inevitably increase, for in Asia lie our great allies as well as our toughest competitors in virtually all arenas of global interest. Domestically, the role of Asian immigrants is more visible than at any other time in our history. In spite of these connections with Asia, however, our knowledge about this crucial region is far from adequate. For various reasons, Asia remains for most of us a relatively unfamiliar, if not stereotypical or even mysterious, "Oriental" land.

There are compelling reasons for Americans to obtain some level of concrete knowledge about Asia. It is one of the world's richest reservoirs of culture and an ever-evolving museum of human heritage. Rhoads Murphey, a prominent Asianist, once pointed out that in the part of Asia east of Afghanistan and south of Russia alone lies half the world, "half of its people and far more than half of its historical experience, for these are the oldest living civilized traditions." Prior to the modern era, with limited interaction and mutual influence between the East and the West, Asian civilizations developed largely independent from the West. In modern times, however, Asia and the West have come not only into close contact but also into frequent conflict: The result has been one of the most solemn and stirring dramas in world history. Today, integration and compromise are the trend in coping with cultural differences. The West—with some notable exceptions—has started to see Asian traditions, not as something to fear, but as something to be understood, appreciated, and even cherished. After all, Asian traditions are an indispensable part of the human legacy, a matter of global "common wealth" that few of us can afford to ignore.

As a result of Asia's enormous economic development since World War II, we can no longer neglect the study of this vibrant region. Japan's "economic miracle" of postwar development is no longer unique, but in various degrees has been matched by the booming economy of many other Asian countries and regions. The rise of the four "mini dragons" (South Korea, Taiwan, Hong Kong, and Singapore) suggests that there may be a common Asian pattern of development. At the same time, each economy in Asia has followed its own particular trajectory. Clearly, China is the next giant on the scene. Sweeping changes in China in the last two decades have already dramatically altered the world's economic map. Furthermore, growth has also been dramatic in much of Southeast Asia. Today war-devastated Vietnam shows great enthusiasm for joining the "club" of nations engaged in the world economy. And in South Asia, India, the world's largest democracy, is rediscovering its role as a champion of market capitalism. The economic development of Asia presents a challenge to Americans but also provides them with unprecedented opportunities. It is largely against this background that more and more people in the United States, in particular among the younger generation, have started to pursue careers dealing with Asia.

This series is designed to meet the need for knowledge of Asia among students and the general public. Each book is written in an accessible and lively style by an expert (or experts) in the field of Asian studies. Each book focuses on the culture and customs of a country or region. Each volume starts with an introduction to the land and people of a nation or region and includes a brief history and an overview of the economy. This is followed by chapters dealing with a variety of topics that piece together a cultural panorama, such as thought, religion, ethics, literature and art, architecture and housing, cuisine, traditional dress, gender, courtship and marriage, festivals and leisure activities, music and dance, and social customs and lifestyle. In this series, we have chosen not to elaborate on elite life, ideology, or detailed questions of political structure and struggle, but instead to explore the world of common people, their sorrow and joy, their pattern of thinking, and their way of life. It is the culture and customs of the majority of the people (rather than just the rich and powerful elite) that we seek to understand. Without such understanding, it will be difficult for all of us to live peacefully and fruitfully with each other in this increasingly interdependent world.

As the world shrinks, modern technologies have made all nations on earth "virtual" neighbors. The expression "global village" not only reveals the nature and the scope of the world in which we live but also, more importantly, highlights the serious need for mutual understanding of all peoples on our planet. If this series serves to help the reader obtain a better understanding of the "half of the world" that is Asia, the authors and I will be well rewarded.

Hanchao Lu
Georgia Institute of Technology

Preface

The title of this volume, *Culture and Customs of Japan*, might imply that it contains information on traditional Japanese culture and customs that are distinct from European or American culture and customs. If it were to discuss only those aspects of Japanese culture that are different from Western culture, this volume would present an image that is far from the reality of Japan today. During the past 130 or so years, Japanese society has gone through a major transformation and in many respects has become like any other industrialized country. This was a result of conscious efforts to modernize the country after the Western model. After all, the West has been the frontrunner in industrialization in the modern age, and various elements of Western culture inevitably have become a part of Japanese culture.

To describe the culture and customs of contemporary Japan that are not exclusive to a small number of elite but shared by ordinary people in daily life is the mission of this book. Most daily activities of the Japanese are already familiar to readers in the United States or other industrialized countries. The everyday life of average people who live in urban areas of Japan consists of being woken up by the alarm clock in the morning, getting dressed in business suits, eating a quick breakfast of toast with milk or coffee while glancing at the daily newspaper, and at the same time watching the morning news on television. They walk or pedal a bicycle to the nearest train station and ride on a train packed with many other commuters for at least half an hour. At their work place (a business office or factory) they share an entire section of a large room with many fellow workers and supervisors. For lunch most of them eat at the employee dining hall, but sometimes they go out to restaurants nearby, possibly to McDonald's. At the end of the work day, fellow workers occasionally go out together for a drink on their way home. Later they are usually too tired to do anything but watch television. When they manage to take a vacation for a few days, many young people travel abroad on package tours. Families with children like to go to beaches or resorts at hot springs.

Whereas attendance at traditional theater productions used to be a popular form of entertainment, only a very small number of people go to traditional theater today. Classical theater of *noh* and *kabuki* belongs to high culture now. It is costly and requires some training on the part of audience members to be able to enjoy it. Still, ordinary people do know something about traditional theater and the names of famous *kabuki* actors whose faces are familiar from television.

The Japanese today have the same type of limited knowledge of classic literature. Not many people would have read the entire story of the 54-volume *Tale of Genji*, but its hero and heroines are very familiar to average people. Moreover, the rhythms of Japanese language expressed in classic poems still resonate today. Favorite lines used by contemporary popular entertainers naturally fit in the rhythm patterns of classic poetry. Thus the entries for literature and theater in this volume are fairly extensive.

Japanese society and culture experienced a radical transformation after the opening of the country to the outside world in the mid-nineteenth century and again during the military occupation following the Pacific War. At present in the post–Cold War world, another restructuring of Japanese society has been under way. Unlike the previous two times, for this round of restructuring Japan does not have a clear model to follow, and it is hard to predict the outcome.

Members of the generation born after Japan became an affluent country think and behave differently from their elders who grew up during or immediately after World War II. The older generation was brought up to respect the virtue of hard work, thrift, and responsibility to the group to which one belongs. The new generation is said to be more individualistic and even irresponsible. Puzzled by the younger generation's behavior, the older generation has called them *shin jinrui* (neo-Homo sapiens), a term that was widely circulated in the 1980s. The new generation perceives Japanese culture and customs quite differently from the older people.

The culture and customs described in this volume reflect the world view of the generation who lived in the early twentieth century when the norms and standards inherited from the feudal past guided individuals' behavior. I myself was born in Tokyo in 1937. When World War II ended in the Pacific in 1945, my family was living in Sendai, the largest city in the northeastern region. At the very end of the war, a large part of the city was burned down in an air raid. My family moved to Kyushu, where my mother had grown up. We descended on the spacious, old house of my grandmother in a farming village on the outskirts of Ogi (a small castle town), where Lord Nabeshima maintained his mansion and enormous garden that later became the public garden of the town.

During the years in Ogi, I had valuable experiences in the life of an old farming village. This was before postwar development touched the area. I was able to catch small fish in bamboo basket traps in a stream that ran through the village. (This stream had been covered by a concrete lid to expand the road by the time I visited twenty years later.) Village children were allowed to participate in (and expected to observe to learn) activities in the community, of which many members were related to each other. Being a curious city kid, I peeked in at all sorts of events taking place in the village, such as meetings for distribution of rationed goods, festivals, weddings, and funerals. I was allowed to experience the feeling of walking bare-foot in the rice paddy to experiment with rice planting. Thanks to these experiences, I can understand literature about Japanese village life in the past much better.

I went to high school and college in Tokyo during the 1950s, when Japan was heading toward rapid economic development. At that time not many people imagined that Japan would become the second-largest economy in the world. Even when I was a graduate student in the United States in the 1960s, I could not imagine such a possibility. When the late Professor Edwin O. Reischauer prophesied that Japan was becoming a major economic power of the world and that it would have much more influence on the United States than China, I could not truly believe him. In the 1969 documentary film *The Japanese*, which Professor Reischauer made in cooperation with Japan Broadcasting Corporation, he stated that in the history of world civilization occasionally a small country has exerted enormous influence on others, like Greece in its golden age, and that Japan may be entering into its golden age. Now I know that he was right. This documentary film captures the culture and society of Japan, as I know it, better than any other films I have seen.

The golden age of modern Japan may be ending with its economic crisis of the 1990s. I have visited Japan every year since 1971 trying to keep up with new developments there. Each time I return to Japan, I find myself bewildered by changes in Japanese language—especially the new expressions in the speech of radio announcers. New words are often created as an abridgment of English words. I realize that I am becoming an old-timer. A friend once teased me, saying that I sounded like a Japanese who lived during the Meiji period. This is the limitation of my ability to illustrate the contemporary culture of Japan for this volume. Readers should not expect to find in this volume the hottest fashions among the teenagers of Japan today. Another warning: I did not try to make this volume a comprehensive compendium covering every aspect of traditional and modern Japanese culture and custom. This can be found elsewhere. Rather, I tried to reflect my personal observations of life in Japan.

I would like to thank my friends in Tokyo who helped me over many years in updating my knowledge on culture and customs in Japan. Without their kind advice, I would not have been able to gather the necessary information for this volume. I am thankful to my colleagues at the University of Michigan at Dearborn for their moral support. The fund from the Campus Grant enabled me to include the map of principal cities in modern Japan in this volume. Also, I would like to thank Lu Hanchao, the editor of this series. The table of contents he suggested was sensibly selective and attractive enough to entice me into writing this volume. It was a good opportunity for me to write down the kind of information on daily life in Japan that my students cannot easily find in their textbooks.

AUTHOR'S NOTE

In Japanese the family name comes first, and the given name follows. For example, MINAMOTO Yoritomo is the full name of a man whose family name is Minamoto and whose given name is Yoritomo. For some ancient names, the word "*no*" is inserted in between the family and given names. For example, Minamoto no Yoritomo means Yoritomo of the Minamoto family. In modern days, Japanese names used in the English-speaking world are normally presented in the same order as in English, with the given name first.

In this volume, Japanese names are given in the Japanese way with the family name first. To avoid confusion, the family names are capitalized when they appear for the first time in the text.

Chronology of the History of Japan

MAJOR PERIODS

Jomon period (ca. 10,000 B.C.–ca. 300 B.C.)

Yayoi period (ca. 300 B.C.–ca. A.D. 300)

Kofun (Tomb) period (ca. A.D. 300–ca. 500)

   Yamato period (ca. 300–710)

      Asuka period (593–710; or 593–628)

      Hakuho period (645–710; or 672–686)

Nara period (710–794)

   Tempyo period (729–748)

Heian period (794–1185)

   Fujiwara era (858–1185)

Kamakura period (1185–1333)

   Kemmu Restoration of the Go-Daigo emperor (1333–1335)

Muromachi (Ashikaga) period (1336–1573)

   Sengoku (The Warring States) period (1467–1568)

   Azuchi-Momoyama period (1568–1600)

Edo (Tokugawa) period (1600–1868)

   Genroku period (1688–1704)

Meiji period (1868–1912)
Taisho period (1912–1926)
Showa period (1926–1989)
Heisei period (1989–   )

CHRONOLOGY

ca. 10,000 B.C.–ca. 300 B.C.	Jomon culture
ca. 300 B.C.–ca. A.D. 300	Yayoi culture
A.D. 57	Envoy to the Chinese Han Court from the Japanese Kingdom of Na (or Nu)
ca. 300–ca. 500	Kofun (Tomb) Culture
ca. 300–710	The Yamato Court in the Yamato Plain
552	The traditional date of the official introduction of Buddhism from Paekche (Korea)
593–622	Prince Shotoku as regent (*sessho*) of the Suiko emperor
604	The Seventeen-Article Constitution
607	Ono-no Imoko goes on the first embassy of Japan to China under the Sui Dynasty
645	Taika Reform
702	Taiho Code is promulgated
708	The first issue of copper coinage
710	Establishment of the first permanent capital, Heijo-kyo (Nara)
712	*Kojiki* (Records of Ancient Matters)
720	*Nihongi* (Chronicles of Japan)
751	*Kaifuso*, the first collection of Chinese verse by Japanese poets
752	Dedication of the Great Buddha at the Todaiji in Nara

738–756	Compilation of *Man'yoshu* (Ten Thousand Leaves), an anthology of poems
784	Capital moves to Nagaoka
788	Saicho founds a temple (Enryakuji) on Mt. Hiei (Kyoto prefecture), the headquarters of the Tendai sect of Buddhism in Japan
794	Inauguration of the capital, Heian-kyo (Kyoto)
816	Kukai founds Kongobuji at Mt. Koya (Wakayama prefecture), the headquarters of the Shingon sect of Buddhism in Japan
838	Last official embassy to China under the Tang Dynasty, led by priest Ennin
858–872	Fujiwara Yoshifusa becomes regent (*sessho*) of the imperial family
894	Official termination of embassy to China by the proposal of Sugawara Michizane
905	*Kokin (waka) shu* compiled by Ki no Tsurayuki and others
941	Fujiwara Tadahira, the regent, becomes the chancellor (*kanpaku*)
972	Kuya (903–972), early popularizer of devotion to Amida Buddha, dies
995–1027	Fujiwara Michinaga (d. 1027) in power; height of the Fujiwara era
ca. 1002	*Makura no soshi* (Pillow Book) of Sei Shonagon
ca. 1002–1019	*Genji monogatari* (The Tale of Genji) by Murasaki Shikibu
1053	Byodoin (a temple) erected by Fujiwara Yorimichi

1086	Shirakawa emperor abdicates and establishes *insei* (rule from the cloister by a retired emperor)
1156	Hogen Insurrection in Kyoto; *samurai* (warriors) play major role in politics
1159	Heiji War; Taira no Kiyomori and his son, Shigemori, triumph over Minamoto Yoshitomo and Fujiwara Nobuyori
1160–1185	Taira clan (Heike) exerts dominance in imperial court
1180–1185	Gempei Wars between Minamoto clan (Genji) and Taira clan (Heike); triumph of Minamoto Yoritomo
1185	Minamoto Yoritomo establishes system of *shugo* (protector) and *jito* (steward)
1192	Minamoto Yoritomo is granted title of *seii taishogun (shogun)* by the emperor
1199	Yoritomo's death; beginning of regency (*shikken*) by his wife, Hojo Masako, and father-in-law, Hojo Tokimasa
1212	Honen, founder of the Jodoshu (Pure Land sect) of Buddhism, dies
1221	Shokyu (Jokyu) disturbance; retired emperor Go-Toba attempts to recover political control
1224–1242	Hojo Yasutoki is *shikken* of the Kamakura *bakufu* (military government)
1227	Dogen returns from China and founds Zen (Soto branch) Buddhism
1232	Promulgation of *Joei Shikimoku* (Joei Code) by Kamakura *bakufu*
1253	Nichiren declares foundation of the Nichiren sect of Buddhism

1262	Shinran, founder of the Jodo Shinshu (True Pure Land), or Shin sect, of Buddhism, dies
1274	Mongol forces attack on Hakata Bay, northern Kyushu, for the first time
1281	Second Mongol attack
ca. 1331	*Tsurezuregusa* (Essays in Idleness) by Yoshida Kenko
1333	Ashikaga Takauji captures Kyoto in Go-Daigo emperor's name; inauguration of direct imperial rule under Go-Daigo; end of the Kamakura *bakufu*
1335	Revolt of Ashikaga Takauji against Go-Daigo emperor
1336	Go-Daigo emperor flees to Yoshino; rival emperor reigns in Kyoto under the protection of Ashikaga Takauji; division of imperial court between northern court (Kyoto) and southern court (Yoshino) until 1392
1338	Ashikaga Takauji assumes title of shogun
1339	*Jinno shoto-ki* (Records of the Legitimate Succession of the Divine Sovereign) by Kitabatake Chikafusa
1368–1394	Ashikaga Yoshimitsu as shogun fosters diplomatic and trade ties with China; after his death Kitayama palace (his villa in Kyoto) becomes the site of Rokuonji, the Temple of the Golden Pavilion, representative of the Kitayama cultural epoch
1384	Kan'ami, who developed *noh* drama, dies
1443	Seami (Zeami), who completed *noh* drama, dies
1443–1473	Ashikaga Yoshimasa as shogun, known to be dominated by his wife, Hino Tomiko. After

retirement he builds his villa in Higashi-yama in Kyoto and patronizes artists. Zen culture—such as *shoin-zukuri* (studio-style residential architecture), tea ceremony, flower arrangement, landscape painting, *yamato-e* (Japanese-style painting), and *noh* drama—flourishes under his patronage. His villa becomes the site of Jishoji, the Zen temple with "Silver Pavilion," a symbol of the Higashiyama cultural epoch.

1467–1477	Onin War; beginning of the era of civil war known as the Warring States period, which lasts until 1568
1543	Arrival of Portuguese at Tanegashima, an island off the southern tip of Kyushu; firearms are introduced
1549	St. Francis Xavier arrives at Kagoshima; does missionary work until he leaves Japan in 1551
1560	Battle of Okehazama; Oda Nobunaga's victory over Imagawa Yoshimoto
1568	Oda Nobunaga controls the capital
1573	Oda Nobunaga expels the last Ashikaga shogun; end of the Ashikaga (Muromachi) *bakufu*
1575	Battle of Nagashino; joint forces of Oda Nobunaga and Tokugawa Ieyasu defeat Takeda Katsuyori; first effective use of firearms in battle
1576	Oda Nobunaga builds his castle at Azuchi on Lake Biwa
1582	Oda Nobunaga's death at the hands of Akechi Mitsuhide; Toyotomi Hideyoshi succeeds to power; beginning of land survey commissioned by Hideyoshi

1587	Hideyoshi orders expulsion of Christian missionaries
1588	Hideyoshi's decree of "Sword Hunt" (confiscation of arms of peasantry); separation of warriors and peasantry
1592	Hideyoshi's first expedition to Korea
1597	Hideyoshi's second expedition to Korea
1598	Hideyoshi dies
1600	Victory of Tokugawa Ieyasu at the Battle of Sekigahara
1603	Tokugawa Ieyasu is granted the title of shogun
1605–1623	Shogunate of Tokugawa Hidetada (d. 1632)
1614, 1615	Seizure of Osaka castle and destruction of Toyotomi Hideyoshi's heirs by Tokugawa Ieyasu
1615	"Laws Governing the Military Households" are promulgated by the Tokugawa *bakufu*
1616	Tokugawa Ieyasu dies
1623–1651	Shogunate of Tokugawa Iemitsu
1636	Ban on Japanese travel abroad
1637–1638	Shimabara Revolt
1639	Portuguese are expelled
1641	Dutch traders are confined to Deshima in Nagasaki
1651–1680	Shogunate of Tokugawa Ietsuna
1680–1709	Shogunate of Tokugawa Tsunayoshi
1657	Great Fire in Edo
1688–1704	Genroku era: economic growth and new urban culture featuring novels of Ihara Saikaku

	(d. 1642), drama of Chikamatsu Monzaemon (d. 1653), poems of Matsuo Basho (d. 1644), and wood-block print art of Hishikawa Moronobu (d. 1638)
1697	Dojima Rice Exchange founded in Osaka
1701–1703	Incident of the Forty-Seven Loyal Retainers
1707	Eruption of Mt. Fuji
1716–1745	Shogunate of Tokugawa Yoshimune (d. 1751)
1716	Relaxation of ban on foreign learning
1732	Great Famine
1783–1786	Serious famines and epidemics
1787–1837	Shogunate of Tokugawa Ienari, who institutes reforms of the Kansei era led by Matsudaira Sadanobu
1791–1792	American and Russian ships visit Japan
1793	Russian lieutenant Adam Laxman visits Hokkaido
1798	Motoori Norinaga completes commentary of *Kojiki*
1804–1829	Bunka-Bunsei era: a cultural epoch
1808	British ship *Phaeton* arrives at Nagasaki
1811	Translation bureau for foreign books
1830–1843	Tempo era: economic crises and reform led by Mizuno Tadakuni
1833–1837	Great Famine
1837	Rice riots in Osaka led by Oshio Heihachiro
1846	U.S. warships under Commodore James Biddle at Uraga request opening of Japan to trade

1853	Commodore Matthew C. Perry arrives at Uraga
1854	Perry vists again; conclusion of U.S.-Japan Friendship Treaty (Kanagawa Treaty)
1856	Townsend Harris, first American consul, arrives
1858	Conclusion of U.S.-Japan Commercial Treaty; foreign trading community is established in Yokohama
1860	First Japanese mission to United States
1862	First Japanese mission to Europe
1863	Bombardment of foreign vessels at Shimonoseki; British bombardment of Kagoshima of Satsuma domain in retaliation for antiforeign activities
1866	Satsuma-Choshu agreement to join forces against the shogunate
1866–1867	Shogunate of Tokugawa Yoshinobu (Keiki, d. 1913)
1867	Enthronement of Emperor Mutsuhito (Meiji emperor)
1868	Proclamation of imperial restoration; emperor's "Five Article Charter Oath"; Tokyo (Edo) becomes new capital
1871	Feudal domains are abolished; in November, departure of Iwakura mission for America and Europe (returned in September 1873)
1872	Railway opens between Tokyo and Yokohama
1873	Gregorian calendar is adopted Universal conscription ordinance New land tax system End of ban on Christianity

1876	Prohibition of carrying sword by samurai
1877	Satsuma Rebellion
1879	Beginning of elected prefectural assemblies
1881	Constitution and parliament are promised for ten years later
1884	Creation of peerage
1885	Adoption of cabinet system with Ito Hirobumi as first premier
1889	February 11: promulgation of Meiji Constitution
1890	July 1: first election for Diet October 30: Imperial Rescript on Education
1894–1895	Sino-Japanese war; Treaty of Shimonoseki
1900	Dispatch of troops to Beijing during Boxer Uprising for protection of legation staff
1902	Anglo-Japanese alliance
1904–1905	Russo-Japanese war; Treaty of Portsmouth
1910	Annexation of Korea Kotoku Shusui's alleged plot to assassinate the emperor
1912	July 30: death of Meiji emperor; accession of son, Yoshihito
1914	August 31: Japan declares war on Germany (World War I)
1915	Twenty-one demands on China are presented to Yuan Shikai
1918	Hara Takashi (Kei), president of Seiyukai, becomes premier
1921	Washington Conference Formation of Japan Communist Party

1923	Great earthquake of Kanto
1925	March: Universal manhood suffrage
1926	December 25: death of Taisho emperor; accession of his son, Hirohito
1931	September 18: Manchurian incident
1932	Inauguration of Manchukuo in Manchuria
1936	February 26: Attempted coup d'état by First Division of the Army
1937	July 7: Marco Polo Bridge incident; outbreak of war with China
1938	April: National Mobilization Law
1939	September 1: Outbreak of war in Europe (World War II)
1940	September: entrance of Japanese troops into French Indo-China; Tripartite Alliance with Germany and Italy October: inauguration of Imperial Rule Assistance Association
1941	Occupation of southern Indo-China December 7: attack on Pearl Harbor; beginning of Pacific War
1942	November: Greater East Asia Ministry is created
1945	July 26: Potsdam Declaration April–June: Okinawa campaign May 8: Germany surrenders August 6: Atomic bomb is dropped on Hiroshima August 8: USSR declares war on Japan; atomic bomb is dropped on Nagasaki August 14: Japan accepts terms of Potsdam Declaration September 2: formal surrender is received on board USS *Missouri*

1945–1951	Occupation by Allied Powers under Supreme Commander, General Douglas MacArthur
1946	Emperor's public denial of his own divinity; Land Reform Act
1947	May 3: promulgation of New Constitution
1951	September: Peace Treaty signed with forty-eight nations; U.S.-Japan Security Pact
1956	Treaty for Normalization with USSR; Japan is admitted to United Nations
1960	Treaty of Mutual Security and Cooperation with United States
1964	Tokyo Olympiad; Japan joins Organization for Economic Cooperation and Development (OECD)
1972	Normalization of relations with China; Okinawa reverts to Japanese administration
1978	Peace treaty with China
1985	Equal Employment Opportunity Law
1987	Japan National Railways is privatized
1989	January 7: Showa emperor dies; his son, Akihito, ascends throne as Heisei emperor
1993	Majority rule of Liberal Democratic Party ends and coalition government follows
1998	Winter Olympic Games in Nagano

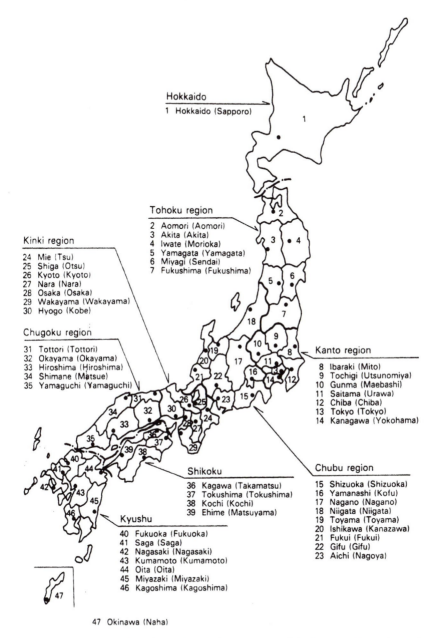

Hokkaido
1 Hokkaido (Sapporo)

Tohoku region
2 Aomori (Aomori)
3 Akita (Akita)
4 Iwate (Morioka)
5 Yamagata (Yamagata)
6 Miyagi (Sendai)
7 Fukushima (Fukushima)

Kinki region
24 Mie (Tsu)
25 Shiga (Otsu)
26 Kyoto (Kyoto)
27 Nara (Nara)
28 Osaka (Osaka)
29 Wakayama (Wakayama)
30 Hyogo (Kobe)

Chugoku region
31 Tottori (Tottori)
32 Okayama (Okayama)
33 Hiroshima (Hiroshima)
34 Shimane (Matsue)
35 Yamaguchi (Yamaguchi)

Kanto region
8 Ibaraki (Mito)
9 Tochigi (Utsunomiya)
10 Gunma (Maebashi)
11 Saitama (Urawa)
12 Chiba (Chiba)
13 Tokyo (Tokyo)
14 Kanagawa (Yokohama)

Chubu region
15 Shizuoka (Shizuoka)
16 Yamanashi (Kofu)
17 Nagano (Nagano)
18 Niigata (Niigata)
19 Toyama (Toyama)
20 Ishikawa (Kanazawa)
21 Fukui (Fukui)
22 Gifu (Gifu)
23 Aichi (Nagoya)

Shikoku
36 Kagawa (Takamatsu)
37 Tokushima (Tokushima)
38 Kochi (Kochi)
39 Ehime (Matsuyama)

Kyushu
40 Fukuoka (Fukuoka)
41 Saga (Saga)
42 Nagasaki (Nagasaki)
43 Kumamoto (Kumamoto)
44 Oita (Oita)
45 Miyazaki (Miyazaki)
46 Kagoshima (Kagoshima)

47 Okinawa (Naha)

Japan's prefectures and prefectural capitals. Courtesy of the Foreign Press Center/ Japan. *Facts and Figures of Japan, 1995.* Copyright © 1995 by the Foreign Press Center/Japan. Used with permission.

Principal cities of modern Japan. From Pyle, Kenneth B. *The Making of Modern Japan,* Second Edition. Copyright © 1996 by Houghton Mifflin Company. Used with permission.

1

Introduction

THE LAND AND PEOPLE

Geography

Japan is an archipelago that stretches almost 2,000 miles in the Pacific Ocean off the northeast to the southwest coasts of the Asian continent. It consists of four main islands, the Ryukyu chain of islands, and over 3,000 smaller islands. The northernmost island, Hokkaido, faces Sakhalin Island of Russia. The main island, Honshu, is the largest and stretches over 1,200 miles from the strait of Tsugaru on the northeast to the strait of Shimonoseki on the southwest. Across these straits Honshu is connected by underground tunnels with Hokkaido (Seikan Tunnel) and Kyushu (Kanmon Tunnel). The island of Shikoku is located off the southwestern shores of Honshu and faces the northwestern tip of Kyushu. The Inland Sea (Seto naikai), the channel between Honshu and Shikoku with numerous tiny islands, is known for its scenic beauty. Shikoku is connected with Honshu by the Great Bridge of Seto, a network of six bridges that stretches about six miles hopping on the islets. The Ryukyu chain of islands (Okinawa is the largest among them) stretches over 1,000 miles between Kyushu and Taiwan.

Japan is a mountainous country. Mountain ranges run through each of the main islands, leaving small plains along the coasts. For this reason, flat land suitable for cultivation constitutes less than 15 percent of the entire country. Countless mountains and waterfalls give scenic beauty to the land, which nurtured the Japanese people's artistic sensibility and religious sentiment from ancient times. There are numerous volcanoes. Mt. Fuji, the highest and venerated for its sublime beauty, has been dormant since 1707. Throughout Japan, frequent earthquakes are caused by volcanic activities as well as by the movement of ocean floors around the country. The great Tokyo earthquake of 1923 took the lives of 142,800 people. The earthquake that hit Kobe in 1995 claimed 6,300 lives.

Climate

The climate of Japan resembles that of the eastern coast of the United States. It ranges from subarctic in the northernmost areas of Hokkaido to subtropical on the islands of Ryukyu. In most of Japan, it is hot and humid in summer and mildly cold in winter. The climate of Tokyo, Japan's capital city, resembles that of Washington, D.C.

The four seasons in most of Japan are quite even and regular, and there is a distinct climate for each season. A pattern of daily life developed to follow the change of seasons in terms of clothing, food preparation, decoration of homes, and even design of letterhead. The monsoons (seasonal winds) with moisture from the south seas in summer and from Siberia in winter are the major factors in the changes of climate. The summer monsoon brings plenty of rain, which is necessary for cultivation of rice, the primary crop of Japan.

The Pacific side of Honshu is blessed by a warm climate that allows good-quality rice to grow in summer and wheat in winter. From the northeast to the southwest, the largest cities of Japan—Sendai, Tokyo, Yokohama, Nagoya, Kyoto, Osaka, Sakai, Kobe, and Hiroshima—developed in this most prosperous zone. Whereas the sunny Pacific coasts are called the "front side of Japan," the gloomy Japan Sea side is identified as the "back side of Japan," where industries and big cities are less developed. Winter monsoons cross the Sea of Japan bringing wet and heavy snow that buries the northern part of the Japan Sea coastal area during the long winter.

Size

The total area of Japan (145,825 square miles) is a little less than that of California. It is, however, larger than any of the European countries except France. Populationwise, Japan had about 125 million inhabitants in the mid-1990s, half that of the United States. Over one-tenth of the total population is concentrated in the greater Tokyo-Yokohama metropolitan area, the hub of Japan's highly centralized economic, political, and cultural activities.

Isolation in the Past

To fly from Washington, D.C., to Tokyo in a jumbo jet takes only twelve hours. Before the age of modern transportation, however, Japan was an isolated country. Its distance from the Asian continent and from the rest of the world had a crucial influence over the formation of Japanese society and culture. At the closest point between Kyushu and Korea, the Tsushima straits separate Japan from the Asian continent for about 100 miles. This distance is about five times greater than that between England and the European continent at Dover. Moreover, strong ocean currents in the straits between Kyushu and Korea make navigation very difficult. Owing to this water barrier, Japan was spared military conquest by continental powers. Two major attempts at military invasion were made by the Mongols, who had built an empire including China and Korea. The Mongols aimed to conquer Japan; however, both attempts failed because their expeditionary forces were hit by a typhoon each time.

Yet Japan was located close enough to the Asian continent to be influenced by the highly advanced civilization of China, which affected the development of ancient culture in Japan. The Chinese and Koreans who migrated to the Japan archipelago in ancient times brought rice cultivation, metallurgy, and other advanced technology. The Japanese adopted the Chinese writing system for their own language, which belongs to a different family from that of Chinese. Until modern times, Chinese classics formed the core curriculum in education of the elite. Confucian philosophy, Chinese-style bureaucracy, Chinese architecture and fine arts, and Chinese cuisine developed in Zen monasteries, and many other elements of ancient Chinese culture influenced the Japanese profoundly. Indeed, Japanese culture was shaped by Chinese and Korean influences throughout its history until Western Europe became its model for modernization in the late nineteenth century.

Ethnic Homogeneity

Japan has long been known as a country inhabited by homogeneous ethnic groups with very similar cultures. Indeed, in comparison with the United States, which is a diverse society of relatively recent migrants from all over the world, Japan is extremely homogeneous. With the exception of a very small minority, the Japanese people believe they descended from ancestors who lived in the country from time immemorial. In fact, migration to the Japan archipelago from the Asian continent and Southeast Asia ended in prehistoric times. Thus the Japanese share many physical features with Asian peoples identified as Mongoloid. Today the similarity in physical features, as well as social norms that emphasize the importance of conformity, create a common pattern of behavior among the Japanese.

Yet there are some small groups of ethnic minorities in Japan. The Ainu ("human," in their own language), who live mostly in Hokkaido, are in some respects descendants of the early inhabitants who had their own language and culture. From around the thirteenth century, they were conquered by the people who settled in the central part of Japan's main island. Today there are only about 20,000 Ainu, and efforts are being made to restore their language and orally transmitted literature.

Okinawans or Ryukyuans who live in the Ryukyu archipelago also once had their own cultural tradition but now have been assimilated into the majority culture of Japan. There are just as many theories on the relationship between the Japanese and Ryukyu cultures as there are on the origins of the Japanese themselves. Around the fourteenth century three kingdoms were formed in Ryukyu; these were united in 1429 by the ruler of the kingdom of Ryukyu, which prospered from interregional trade in the East China Sea. In the early seventeenth century the kingdom was subjugated by Satsuma, a feudal domain in southern Kyushu. When Japan was united under a central government in Tokyo in the mid-nineteenth century, Ryukyu was annexed as a part of Japanese territory, Okinawa prefecture. After the Pacific War it was placed under U.S. administration until 1972, when it reverted to Japan. The Okinawan people are very proud of their distinct cultural tradition. At the same time, they are sensitive about equality with people in other prefectures in Japan because of a history of discrimination against the Okinawans. In the 1990s, the major issue between Okinawa and the rest of the country has been that over 75 percent of the U.S. military bases in Japan are concentrated on Okinawa, causing it to carry a disproportionately large share of the burden.

Among minorities of foreign origins, Koreans are the largest group at about 700,000. For the most part they are the offspring of laborers who were brought over during World War II from Korea, which was under Japan's colonial rule. There are also communities of Chinese who came from Taiwan, another colonial territory of Japan before 1945.

People who were born in the families of outcasts of the feudal past are identified as *burakumin* (people of the [special] hamlet), a euphemistic term. They account for between 1 and 2 percent of the population and used to be engaged in occupations such as leather work or butchery. Despite efforts to eliminate prejudice against them, social discrimination against this "invisible" group has continued.

Important Cultural Centers

Tokyo is more than the political center of Japan with the Diet (parliament), central government bureaucracy including national police headquarters, and the supreme court. (The imperial palace, the symbolic center of Japan, occupies a huge area in the center of the metropolis.) Tokyo is also the center of Japan's economy. Most of the big business corporations have headquarters in Tokyo, and even local businesses and banks maintain liaison offices there. The largest stock exchange market is in Tokyo. Yokohama, which is contiguous to Tokyo, is the largest port in Japan. The nation's largest and busiest international airport, Narita Airport, is connected to Tokyo by highways and express trains. The city also dominates the country's cultural life. The Japanese spoken language is standardized after that of Tokyo. The semi-government broadcasting corporation, NHK (Nippon Hoso Kyokai), which dominates nationwide television and radio broadcasting, is centered in Tokyo. The major newspapers published in Tokyo are distributed throughout the country. The greatest number of universities are concentrated in Tokyo; this includes the National University of Tokyo, which ranks top in Japan's academic hierarchy. Tokyo also attracts the most talented artists, writers, performers, and professionals who aspire to gain a national reputation. In other words, Japan is a uni-centered country.

The entire region, with Tokyo and Yokohama on its coast, is identified as the Kanto (east of the pass) region, as it is located in the Kanto Plain. The largest in Japan, this plain stretches 120 miles at its longest point. The area, including Tokyo, developed as the political and cultural center of Japan relatively late in history, only after Edo (present-day Tokyo) became the seat of the *shogun*'s government in 1603.

The Kansai (west of the pass) region, which centers around Kyoto, Osaka, Nara, and Kobe, is the second-largest metropolitan area. This region has a much longer history as the political, economic, and cultural center than the Kanto area. During the Tokugawa era, Osaka was the hub of the nationwide market system and monetary economy. Residents of Kansai are extremely proud of their cultural heritage, from the Kansai dialect to Kansai-style *sushi*. The Kanto and the Kansai are two great cultural rivals.

Nagoya, the third-largest metropolis, which developed from a castle town midway between the Kanto and the Kansai, is the center of a region identified as Central Japan. To the west of the Kansai, the cities of Okayama and Hiroshima are located on the coastal areas of the Inland Sea, which stretches between Honshu and Shikoku. Hakata and Nagasaki in northern Kyushu are cities with distinct histories. The cities of Kumamoto and Kagoshima in central and southern Kyushu were castle towns of the regional lords and are endowed with a rich heritage from the feudal past.

There are many cities with rich cultural legacies on the Japan Sea coast, such as Izumo and Kanazawa, and in the northern part of Honshu, as well as in Hokkaido. Naha, the administrative center of Okinawa prefecture, was once the capital city of the king of Ryukyu, before Okinawa was annexed to Japan in the mid-nineteenth century. Okinawa and each of the islands of Ryukyu archipelago have distinctive features of subtropical culture. Ryukyu culture also reflects its historical tie with China, especially in music, dance, fabrics, and cuisine.

During the era of postwar economic growth in the mid-twentieth century, many young people left their home towns seeking greater opportunities in Tokyo and the other metropolitan areas. A recent trend is the reverse flow of people, which is known as the "U-turn" phenomenon. Since the 1980s there has been an effort to enhance greater local autonomy in economic and cultural life. In Japan today, many local cities have very modern city halls, libraries, theaters, schools, and other cultural centers designed by world-famous architects.

JAPANESE LANGUAGE

Spoken Language

The Japanese language is classified as one of the Altaic or Ural-Altaic family, which includes Korean, Turkic, and Mongolic languages. These languages have common characteristics: initial consonants are simple, verbs have suffixes, modifiers precede the word modified, and verbs come at the end of sentences. Nevertheless, the differences between modern Japanese and modern Korean are much greater than those between English and Italian.

The model speakers of the standard Japanese are announcers of NHK (Nippon Hoso Kyokai), or Japan Broadcasting Corporation. They are supposed to be the keepers of correct Japanese. The standard spoken language was formulated after the Meiji Restoration of 1868 when Japan became a centralized nation state with a new capital in Tokyo. The leaders of the new government came from different regions of Japan and spoke different dialects. There was need for a standardized language to be spoken by Japanese from all regions and from various social levels in the feudal society. Also, the national language had to be suitable for public speeches and instruction in schools. The language spoken in Tokyo became the basis of the standard Japanese. In fact, however, the language actually spoken by genuine Tokyoites, Edokko (Edo is the old name of Tokyo, and Edokko means Tokoites—those who lived in Edo), is not precisely the same as the standard Japanese. Strictly speaking, those who truly deserve to be identified as Edokko are descendants of those who had lived in certain downtown sections on the eastern bank of the Sumida River in Tokyo for at least three generations by the early twentieth century. The area was inhabited mostly by artisans, shop-keepers, and their servants. Rich and lively expressions in their language, as well as their peculiar enunciation, are preserved by masters of *kodan, rakugo*, and *manzai*, which are "talk shows" inherited from the Tokugawa period.

Just as any language, changes are taking place constantly in Japanese. New words are either foreign (most often English) terms adapted into the Japanese vocabulary with some adjustment in pronunciation, or newly created words that express new phenomena or concepts.

It is said that Japanese sounds like Italian, at least to some Americans who do not speak Italian. The sound of Japanese is very simple. Each syllable consists of one consonant followed by one vowel. If one can pronounce five basic vowels correctly, one can guess how to pronounce various combinations of consonants and vowels in Japanese words when they are written in the Roman alphabet. These five basic vowels are: *a* (pronounced like *a* in father), *i* (pronounced like *i* in gift), *u* (like *oo* in foot), *e* (like *e* in less), *o* (like *o* in off). For example, a surname "Nose" is pronounced *no-se*, in two syllables.

It is relatively easy for a foreigner to learn how to pronounce Japanese words and put them together to make simple sentences; however, it is more difficult to choose appropriate words for a certain circumstance. To make a simple statement, there are many possible expressions. One has to choose appropriate words to make a statement in accordance with the person and the circumstance involved.

A Japanese speaker must constantly keep in mind his or her relative po-sition to the other, which is determined by one's social position, age, rela-tionship, or other factors related to the particular circumstance. To make a statement, one has a choice to make it polite or plain, formal or informal, masculine or feminine. The use of honorific or humble (self-deprecatory) expressions may be the most difficult part of learning the Japanese language.

There are many words for "I" to indicate oneself. For a man or a woman, the standard word is "*watakushi*," or in its less formal expression, "*watashi*" or "*atashi*." A man can use "*boku*" in less formal conversation. For a man, "*ore*" or "*washi*" is also possible for informal conversation. In addition, there are old-fashioned expressions and numerous local variations. Moreover, in conversation it is not necessary to mention the word referring to oneself. The word "I" is not mentioned in most real-life conversations, because it is understood from the context. The same for the word "you." There are even more numerous words for "you." In conversations, the word "you" is mentioned only when emphasis is placed on "you," and in most cases "you" is implied by the use of honorific expressions of verbs and other words in the sentence. There are many words meaning "eat," for example.

Written Language

The Japanese adopted the Chinese writing system (probably during the fifth century A.D.) despite the fact that the languages of China and Japan belong to different families of languages. Their sound system, vocabulary, and grammar are very different. Chinese characters (*kanji*) are ideographic and pronounced in one syllable. One Chinese character represents one word. The Japanese devised two sets of pronunciation for each Chinese character. One is very close to the original Chinese pronunciation, which is the *on* reading. The other involves reading a Chinese character in Japanese translation, which is the *kun* reading. For example, a Chinese character that means "water" and is pronounced *shui* in Chinese is read *sui* in the Japanese *on* reading. The same character is read *mizu* (meaning "water" in Japanese) in the *kun* reading.

To write down Japanese in Chinese characters, another device was necessary because of the different grammatical structures of the two languages. Chinese is not inflectional, and therefore words do not change their forms to indicate tense (past, present, or future) or to indicate affirmative or negative. To handle this problem, the Japanese used some Chinese characters to represent Japanese words phonetically. The earliest texts of the history of Japan, *Kojiki* and *Nihongi*, also called *Nihon shoki*, were written partly in Chinese and partly in Japanese by using Chinese characters phonetically. In the earliest anthology of poems, *Man'yoshu*, the phonetic use of Chinese characters was extensive.

Later in the ninth century the Japanese created two sets of *kana*, or Japanese syllabary systems. Each has about fifty phonetic symbols. One of them is *katakana*, and the other is *hiragana*. The *katakana* was developed from a part of a Chinese character, and the *hiragana* was developed from a cursive form of Chinese characters.

Today, three sets of writing systems are used in a single piece of writing in Japanese: namely, *kanji* (Chinese characters), *hiragana*, and *katakana*. *Kanji* is used for most nouns and the stem of verbs, adjectives, and adverbs. The inflectional ending, suffix, grammatical particles, and function words are always written in *hiragana*. *Katakana* is used to represent foreign names and sounds without meaning.

Writing in the modern period has changed from the early twentieth-century preference for many Chinese characters to the current preference for fewer. There are 1,945 Chinese characters in the list approved by the Japanese government for use in publications for the general public and in schools through the end of ninth grade. In addition, there are 284 characters approved for writing personal names. They were chosen from some 50,000 characters listed in the largest Chinese language dictionary. In order to pass as a literate person and enjoy popular literature today, it is necessary for a Japanese citizen to know at least about 3,000 commonly used Chinese characters, which are listed as *tsuyo kanji* (commonly used Chinese characters) in dictionaries.

THE ORIGIN OF JAPAN IN MYTHOLOGY

According to mythological tales recorded in the earliest history of Japan, the islands of Japan were created by a god and goddess named Izanagi and Izanami. Before the heaven and earth were not separated from each other, there was a floating bridge of heaven on which the two gods appeared and together stirred the ocean with a jewel-headed spear. The drippings from the spear formed islands.[1]

After producing each of the islands of Japan, this couple gave birth to the gods of various natural phenomena, such as the wind, mountains, rivers, seas, and trees. Izanami was burned to death when she gave birth to the god of fire. Izanagi chased her to the land of death but was refused by her. At a beach on his way back, Izanagi cleansed himself of death. When he washed his eyes with sea water Amaterasu, the Sun Goddess, was born out of a drop of brine, along with the Moon God and the Storm God. Amaterasu was designated to be the lord of the universe. She sent down her grandchild, Ninigi, to Japan to be its ruler. When Ninigi left she presented him with three treasures—a bronze mirror, a sword, and a curved jade—which are regarded as the imperial regalia of Japan to this day. Ninigi and his companions landed on a high mountain peak in central Kyushu and marched on to Yamato, the central part of the main island, battling and conquering hostile tribes along the way. Eventually in the Yamato Plain, Ninigi's grandson established himself as the Jimmu (Divine Warrior) emperor, the first emperor of Japan. The following is an excerpt from the beginning of *Kojiki* translated in simplified form:

The names of the deities that were born in the Plain of High Heaven when Heaven and Earth began were the deity Master of the Center of Heaven, next the High Producing Wondrous Deity, next the Divine Producing Wondrous Deity. These three deities were all deities born alone, and they hid their persons [i.e., died]. The earth was young and like floating oil, and as it drifted about like a jellyfish something sprouted up like a reed shoot. The names of the deities that were born from it were Pleasant Reed Shoot Deity, followed by the Heavenly and Eternally Standing Deity. . . . next the deity Izanagi ("Male Who Invites"), next his younger sister Izanami ("Female Who Invites"). . . .

Hereupon all the heavenly deities commanded the two deities Izanami and Izanagi to form and consolidate this drifting land and gave them a heavenly jeweled spear. So the two deities, standing upon the Floating Bridge of Heaven, pushed down the jeweled spear and stirred with it. They stirred the brine until it curdled, and then they drew the spear up. The brine that dripped down from the end of the spear piled up and became an island.[2]

Kojiki (Records of Ancient Matters, 3 vols., compiled in A.D. 712) and *Nihon shoki* [also called *Nihongi*] (Chronicles of Japan, 30 vols., compiled in A.D. 720) are the earliest written national histories of Japan. Both were compiled under imperial orders to write down orally transmitted stories, and were written in Chinese characters. As the earliest extant books in Japan, they are also the earliest recorded literature and the earliest source of information on ancient Japanese thought and religion. Each book tells similar stories in different versions and in various degrees of detail. The reason why two books were compiled around the same time is not entirely clear, but it has been speculated that *Nihon shoki* was compiled with greater awareness of the need for proclaiming the foundation of the centralized state of Japan to the outside world (namely, China and kingdoms in Korea) than *Kojiki* was.

Both *Kojiki* and *Nihon shoki* begin with stories of "the age of the gods," which are mythological narratives concerning the beginning of the universe, the creation of the islands of Japan, and the births of the divine rulers who dwelt in Japan. The legends and folklore in these books reflect the process of formation of the state of Japan under a centralized government headed by the imperial family, who emerged after centuries of struggles, conquests, and alliances with marriage ties among powerful regional clans. Various stories explain the mythological origins of the imperial family and the chronicles of emperors from the legendary first emperor, Jimmu emperor, through the thirty-third emperor, Suiko emperor (r. A.D. 592–628) in *Kojiki*, and through the forty-first Jito emperor (r. A.D. 690–697) in *Nihon shoki.*

BRIEF OUTLINE OF JAPANESE HISTORY

Ancient Japan

The Jomon Period (ca. 10,000 B.C.–300 B.C.)

The earliest culture in Japan during the New Stone Age is identified as the Jomon culture, represented by *jomon* (cord-marked) style pottery. The Jomon period lasted from around 10,000 B.C. through around 300 B.C. During this period people lived by fishing, hunting, and gathering nuts, berries, young shoots of plants, and other food provided by nature. Large amounts of shells discovered near the remains of their dwellings suggest that shellfish was an important source of nutrition. To store the nuts, people made earthen jars decorated by rolling straw cord over the surface before firing. They built their houses on a shallow pit, using slanting rafters that formed both the frame of the house and the roof, and covering the roof with bark and grass. Their houses were clustered in large groups, indicating that they lived in communities. They used polished stone, bones of animals, and seashells to make tools and ornaments such as necklaces and bracelets. They made earthen figurines called *dogu* for religious rituals.

By the end of the Jomon period, people began to grow some food— including rice, which later became the staple food. The rice plant originated in Southeast Asia, spread to southern China, and was brought to Japan through Korea. There are strong suggestions that many people migrated from the Chinese continent to Japan and brought advanced culture. It was during the Yayoi period that rice cultivation spread in Japan.

The Yayoi Period (ca. 300 B.C.–A.D. 300)

Yayoi is the name of the ward in Tokyo where archaeologists discovered the site that belonged to this era. Pottery unearthed from this site represents a culture that followed the Jomon. Yayoi pottery is thinner, harder, and lighter than the Jomon, suggesting that Yayoi people had potters' wheels and the technology to fire at higher heat. During the Yayoi period, agriculture— especially rice cultivation—became the mainstay of the economy. The population increased, villages became larger, and powerful leaders expanded their command beyond their own villages, creating larger communities. The leaders lived in houses with elevated floors, which later became a fundamental element of the Japanese house. As a symbol of their political power, the leaders of larger communities built monumental tombs for themselves.

Early Chinese dynastic histories recorded that there were over a hundred states in Japan and that some of them sent envoys to China. An envoy sent by the ruler of the Nakoku (the state of Na) of Japan was received by the Chinese emperor in A.D. 57. As a symbol of recognition of the state, the emperor bestowed on him a gold seal with the inscription, "the seal of the king of Na state of Wa (Japan)." Some 1,700 years later a gold seal, which was identified as the one given by the Chinese emperor, was unearthed in northern Kyushu.

The Tomb Period (ca. A.D. 300–ca. 500)

Because of the proliferation of large tombs, the period following the Yayoi is identified as the *kofun* (ancient tombs) period. The tombs indicate a strong influence by the contemporary Chinese culture, not only in design but also in burial items: bronze swords, bronze bells, bronze mirrors, glazed ceramic ware, and even iron weapons were discovered. The tombs were covered with mounds, around which earthen figurines called *haniwa* were placed. They were in the images of military men, musicians and dancers, falconers, horses, dogs, and other things such as houses. The bottom part of a *haniwa* was a cylinder. These were placed around the mound to prevent soil erosion. Burial items found in the tombs indicate that Japan entered the Bronze Age and Iron Age almost simultaneously when these items were brought from China.

The large burial mounds were found in the western two-thirds of the Japanese islands. The largest among them were located in the Yamato Plain in the Nara basin on the east of Osaka, suggesting that the greatest wealth and power was concentrated in this area. During the third century Himiko, a woman ruler of Japan, sent an envoy to China. The location of her state has long been disputed: some historians believe it was in northern Kyushu, and some maintain it was in the Yamato Plain.

The Yamato Period (ca. A.D. 300–710)

The foundation of the Yamato Court (the rudimentary government located in the Yamato Plain) by the ancestors of the imperial family is estimated to have occurred sometime during the fourth century A.D. From this point on, the chronology of Japanese history is marked by the location of the government in power. Political organization within the country during the Yamato period was still relatively primitive. Most of the land remained under the control of tribal units called *uji*, of which members were bound by real or imagined kinship ties. Over the course of prolonged struggles, these groups sooner or later accepted a subordinate relationship with the ruling group in the Yamato Plain. However, the process of the establishment of the Yamato Court is revealed only in fragmentary records and legends.

By the sixth century, when the Yamato Court was located in the Asuka area of the Yamato Plain, increasing waves of cultural influences arrived from China. The transmission of the text of Buddhist canon and Confucian classics was the most significant. The Japanese began to use the Chinese writing system, as they did not have their own. As a result of China's cultural influence, the Japanese became conscious of their own national identity. At the Yamato Court a fight erupted over the acceptance of Buddhism, a foreign religion transmitted from the Chinese continent. The supporters of Buddhism won out, and Japan continued to regard the continental civilization as an ideal. Prince Shotoku, who served the Suiko emperor (his aunt) as her regent from 593 to 622, promoted Buddhism.[3] He ordered the building of Buddhist temples, including Horyuji near Nara. The Horyuji temple complex is famous for having the oldest wooden buildings extant in the world and beautiful Buddhist statues and wall paintings dating from this era.

Prince Shotoku attempted to shape the government after the model of Chinese system, in which the powerful emperor had control over aristocrats who served the government as bureaucrats. He wrote the "Seventeen-Article Constitution," in essence Buddhist and Confucian moral admonitions with emphasis on the importance of harmony and obedience to the sovereign ruler. In the same spirit, he instituted a Chinese-style official ranking system. He sent a mission to China to learn from the higher civilization there and, at the same time, to assert that Japan was equal to China as an independent nation. The famous sentence in his letter to the Chinese emperor, "the Son of Heaven in the land where the sun rises addresses a letter to the Son of Heaven in the land where the sun sets," reflected Japan's national pride.

After the time of Prince Shotoku, those who promoted reform seized power at the court in 645. The event is known as the Taika Reform. Taika (meaning "grand transformation") was the reign title, or the period name, given to the period from 645 to 649.[4]

The Nara Period (710–794)

In 710 the Chinese-style capital, Heijo-kyo, was completed in Nara. The largest capital city Japan ever had, it was intended to be the permanent capital. The Nara period is characterized by Japan's earnest effort to learn from Chinese civilization. At the time, China under the Tang Dynasty prospered as a great empire. Its cosmopolitan capital, Chang'an, attracted peoples from all over the civilized world—including Mediterranean regions, Persia, and India. The government organizations and code of law were refined to become the foundation of future development. Fine arts, music, and literature enjoyed imperial patronage. Tang China was such an admirable empire that the Japanese government sent successive missions of officials, Buddhist priests, and promising students despite the enormous cost and the danger of navigating the rough seas.

Following the examples set by the Tang Dynasty emperors in China, the Shomu emperor in Japan had a Great Buddha statue constructed in the capital. The height of the sitting Buddha statue is 52 feet. The Todaiji (the East Great Temple) was built to house the Buddha statue. During the Nara period, coin was minted for the first time in Japan after the model of Chinese copper coin. By using the Chinese writing system, the *Kojiki* and *Nihon shoki* were compiled. (Compilation of official history had been a part of China's dynastic tradition.) The compilation of *Man'yoshu*, the earliest anthology of poems under the imperial auspices, also followed the example of Chinese tradition. Moreover, much of the Tang Dynasty law code was adopted.

In economic policy and fiscal administration, the Nara Court adopted the "equal-field" system of the Tang Dynasty model. Under this system all arable land in the country was regarded as belonging to the emperor, and the government distributed equitable portions of land to individual families. In return, families who received the land paid tax. It was an effective system by which to raise revenue for the central government as long as the government could maintain accurate records of land distribution and enforce tax payment.

Chinese influences on Japanese arts and literature were also profound. Much of what Japanese think of as "traditional Japanese" culture in fact had Chinese origins. For example, *gagaku*—the ritual music of the imperial court played by pipe, drum, and stringed instruments made of bamboo and silk— was originally played in the Tang capital of Chang'an and was brought back by Japanese students who studied there. The Japanese, however, did not adopt all aspects of Tang culture. During the Tang Dynasty, the Chinese started to use chairs and beds. But the Japanese have maintained the custom of sitting and sleeping on an elevated floor in the style of Han Dynasty (206 B.C.–A.D. 220) China. Use of chairs and beds in Japan only became common after Western-style buildings were widespread.

The Heian Period (794–1185)

Visitors to Nara today can see how much space the Buddhist temples and monasteries once occupied there. Because the Buddhist establishments acquired too much power and prestige in Nara and the Buddhist clergy became too overbearing, it is said, the capital was moved to Kyoto.

The new capital was named Heian-kyo. Like its predecessor, Heian-kyo was designed as a permanent capital after the Chinese model. Until 1868 when the emperor moved to Tokyo, the imperial palace remained in Kyoto.

To this date at the very end of the twentieth century, the line of the imperial family has continued, and the emperor has remained as the highest authority to legitimate power and prestige in Japan through ritual. In the current constitution of Japan, the emperor is defined as "the symbol of the state and the unity of the people," and he appoints the prime minister as designated by the Diet (parliament.) The highest honor for scholars, artists, writers, and others who contribute to Japanese culture is the "Order of Culture" bestowed on them by the emperor every year.

In terms of political power and functions, however, the emperor was no longer a monarch with absolute power after the early Heian period. Aristocratic families who owned large estates exerted great influence on the imperial court and controlled the succession of the throne. Among them the Fujiwara family, who had roots in an aristocratic clan of the Yamato period and owned the greatest estates, dominated the imperial court as high-ranking officials and regents for the emperors. Princes born to the imperial consorts who came from the Fujiwara family were often chosen as successors to the imperial throne. Because of the domination of the Fujiwara family, the last three hundred years of the Heian period are identified as the Fujiwara era.

The cultural orientation of the Heian period is characterized by Japanization of the imported Chinese culture. By this time the Japanese had lost enthusiasm for learning more from China. In 894 Japan terminated the tradition of sending official missions to China. Instead of trying to copy Chinese style, they created Japanese-style culture by adapting the Chinese model to suit their convenience and taste. It was symbolized in *kana*, the Japanese syllabary system created on the basis of Chinese characters.

The Heian culture was that of the aristocrats who refined the elegant lifestyle centered on rituals at the imperial court in Kyoto, and who cultivated the arts and literature. Heian literature was represented by poems, essays, and novels written in *kana*. *The Tale of Genji*, written by a court lady, Murasaki Shikibu (Lady Murasaki), is regarded as the greatest masterpiece of *kana* literature.

Japan in the Feudal Age

Toward the end of the Heian period the power and authority of the central government declined, and new dynamic groups developed in the provinces. Local magnates dominated the countryside with bands of warriors armed with bow and arrow, curved steel sword, and skill in horseback riding. The origins of these leaders were various. Some were managers of noblemen's estates. Others started as local administrators who were sent to provincial posts as deputies of aristocrats and eventually settled in the local community. The leaders and followers of each group banded together as a family through a pledge of loyalty. They extended networks of alliances with other groups within a large region. They also became involved in the affairs of the central government and power politics in Kyoto. These warriors were known as *samurai* (men in waiting) because they served noblemen in Kyoto as their armed guards, and they became active agents in political strife among the aristocratic families.

Among the warrior families, the Taira clan (or Heike) was the first to rise. They originated in the coastal area of the Inland Sea near Hiroshima. This family moved its headquarters to Kyoto and worked to be accepted into aristocratic circles. As their political strategy, the Tairas followed the pattern of the Fujiwara family to marry their daughters into the imperial family. The family head of Taira who put his grandson on the throne obtained the highest position in the Court.

The powerful rival of the Taira clan was the Minamoto clan (Genji). In the wars of 1156 and 1159 between the two clans, the Tairas defeated the Minamotos. Later, Yoritomo, the heir of the Minamoto leader who built his base in Kamakura in the Kanto region of eastern Japan, defeated the Taira clan by 1185 and became the unchallenged military chief. In 1192 the emperor appointed him *seii taishogun* (generally known as *shogun*), which literally meant "the generalissimo to suppress barbarians"—that is, adversaries of the emperor. From this time on, *shogun* became the highest title given to a warrior who became the actual ruler of Japan during the feudal age.

The Kamakura Period (1185–1333)

MINAMOTO no Yoritomo maintained his headquarters, *bakufu* (literally, "government from the military tent," or the shogunate), in Kamakura, which became the center of control over the whole land. He awarded his warrior followers with fiefs by confiscating the estates of defeated clans, and he appointed them stewards (*jito*) and protectors (*shugo*), newly created positions for local administration. These feudal lords were personally loyal to the Minamoto family and supported the Kamakura bakufu as its mainstay. In theory at least, the Kamakura leaders left the old imperial government intact, and hereditary aristocrats continued to occupy high civil positions, which became less and less effective. The law code of Kamakura bakufu based on local customary law, rather than the old Chinese-style codes of the imperial government, became the guide of judicial administration.

Kamakura-period culture was inspired by new sects of Buddhism, especially the Zen sect. Zen was brought from China as a result of the development of trade. The culture of the Zen monastery was congenial to the stoic self-discipline and frugal lifestyle of the samurai. Patronized by the Kamakura rulers, Zen greatly influenced the elite culture of the new age. The five Zen monasteries of Kamakura still remain as monuments of Kamakura culture. At the same time, evangelist monks of the Pure Land sect of Buddhism spread the faith among commoners and gained a great number of followers, creating a dynamic constituency.

The Kamakura bakufu came to an end in 1333 when the strong-minded Go-Daigo emperor (with the aid of a turncoat Kamakura general, ASHIKAGA Takauji) revolted and declared the restoration of the imperial government. By that time the loyalty of the Kamakura warriors had been eroded. First, the Minamoto family, the focal point of their loyalty, had been discontinued, and the bakufu was being administered by members of the Hojo family (the family of Yoritomo's widow), who created the position of regent for themselves to serve under the figurehead shogun brought from other families related to the imperial family.

The decisive blow to the Kamakura bakufu came in the form of two Mongol invasions. In 1274 and 1281 the rulers of the Mongol empire that ruled China and Korea sent expeditionary forces to subjugate Japan. Fortunately for Japan, the Mongols chose to attack while powerful seasonal storms were hitting northern Kyushu, and the invaders were forced to withdraw. The Japanese regarded these storms, or typhoons, as *kamikaze* (divine wind) that protected the country. However, the cost of defense took a heavy toll on the Kamakura bakufu.

The Muromachi (Ashikaga) Period (1336–1573); the Warring States Period (1467–1568); the Azuchi-Momoyama Period (1568–1600)

The Go-Daigo's new regime was short-lived as Ashikaga Takauji betrayed him and established another member of the imperial family as the emperor in Kyoto. Go-Daigo and his heirs maintained a rival court in the mountains to the south of Kyoto until 1392. Ashikaga Takauji built his headquarters in the Muromachi ward of Kyoto in 1336, which has been identified as the Muromachi bakufu. It continued in Kyoto until 1573. However, after civil war erupted in 1467, it lost control beyond the small areas around Kyoto.

Thereafter for an entire century, incessant civil wars were fought among the warrior clans. This is named the Warring States period. During this time the lords of the early Ashikaga period were mostly replaced by a new breed who dominated over larger areas beyond their own domains. By forcing lords with smaller domains to become their vassals, they established themselves as the *daimyo* (feudal lords). Their ultimate goal was to overpower other lords and put the entire country under lasting control. This task was carried out in succession by three great lords—ODA Nobunaga, TOYOTOMI Hideyoshi, and TOKUGAWA Ieyasu—all of whom came from central Japan around Nagoya, midway between Kyoto and modern Tokyo.

Oda Nobunaga moved his army into Kyoto and put the city under his control in 1568, expelled the Ashikaga shogun, and suppressed various enemies including the monk-soldiers of the Buddhist monastery at Mount Hiei near Kyoto and militant peasant bands who offered tenacious resistance. Just as he began to create a new order, however, he was assassinated by one of his generals. Toyotomi Hideyoshi, Nobunaga's ally who had started as a humble foot soldier, quickly avenged Oda's death and established his hegemony over all lords. He pushed forward Oda Nobunaga's program of "land survey" to measure the agrarian productivity of all the land. The unit of measurement, *koku* (about five bushels), thereafter became the standard unit for assessing the value of farmland. Another significant policy enforced by Hideyoshi was the so-called sword hunt in which farmers in the villages were disarmed and warriors were required to register with their lord, live around the lord's castle, and give up their land in the villages. The purpose was to separate the military households and the farmers in order to prevent new military bands from arising in the countryside. Ever since, the civilian population of Japan have never armed themselves, leaving defense to their government.

Toward the end of his life, Hideyoshi had an ambition to conquer China and sent an expedition to Korea. He died of illness, however, when his forces were stopped by Chinese armies in Korea and the military campaign was stalemated. His invasion is remembered by the Koreans and the Chinese with great resentment and indignation to this day.

The final battle in the long struggle for unification of Japan was fought between two leagues of lords: one was headed by Tokugawa Ieyasu, who was now based at Edo (modern Tokyo) in the Kanto Plain; the other consisted of lords based in the Kansai region centering around Kyoto. In a battle that took place in 1600 at Sekigahara, near Nagoya, Tokugawa Ieyasu emerged as the ultimate victor.

In art history, the final years of the Warring States period are identified as the Azuchi-Momoyama era after the names of the places where Nobunaga and Hideyoshi, respectively, built their castles. Expressing the dynamic spirit of the new age, they sumptuously decorated the great halls of their castles with bold paintings on gold lacquer panel screens.

During this era Spanish and Portuguese traders and Jesuit priests began to appear on Japan's coasts. Firearms (muskets and canons) introduced by the Portuguese, who arrived on the southern tip of Kyushu in 1543, spread rapidly and changed the nature of warfare in Japan. For example, castle buildings with white-walled wooden structures surrounded by moats and stone walls were built. Among the warring lords, Nobunaga was the first to make effective use of firearms. He and many other lords befriended the Jesuit missionaries, who won large numbers of converts in the domains of southwestern Japan.

The Edo (Tokugawa) Period (1600–1868)

Tokugawa Ieyasu was given the title *shogun* by the emperor in 1603 and ruled the country from his headquarters in Edo. His castle was located in the center of modern Tokyo, and its foundation, moat, and stone walls for fortification remain as part of the imperial palace today.

The Tokugawa regime is characterized as a period of "centralized feudalism" because the Tokugawa *bakufu* (shogunate) was capable of extending quite effective control over all the feudal lords (*daimyo*) and functioned very much like centralized governments in the modern era in creating transportation and communication systems, and in enforcing laws. Unlike a central government in the modern age, however, the Tokugawa government could not collect taxes from all over the country. The primary financial resources of the Tokugawas were in their own domains, which amounted to about one-quarter of the farmland of the entire country, major cities including Kyoto and Osaka, mines, and the trading port of Nagasaki. These areas were placed under the direct control of the Tokugawa bakufu. In addition, it was capable of demanding various kinds of services and contributions from the feudal lords.

Altogether there were over 200 lords with various sizes of domains ranging from 10,000 to one million *koku* (a unit of measurement based on approximately five bushels of grain). They were classified into three categories based on their historical relationship with the Tokugawa family. The bakufu controlled the lords by various methods of checks and balances. One was known as "alternate attendance" (*sankin kotai*), which required each lord to personally serve at the shogun's castle in Edo every other year, leaving the administration of his domain in the hands of his retainers. In alternate years when the lord stayed in his own domain, his wife and sons had to stay in Edo under the supervision of the Tokugawa officials. This practice of presenting family members as hostages was standard in making pledges of fealty and political alliances among warriors during the Warring States period.

In Tokugawa society, the samurai and their families (about 6% of the population) had the highest status and privileges as a ruling elite. Symbols of their status included long and short swords, family name, the use of baked roof tiles, and high-quality silk garments. Within the samurai there was another hierarchy. Under the shogun and the daimyo, samurai of various ranks served as retainers in the bakufu and the feudal domains of the lords. Their status was hereditary, and they received annual stipends according to their family rank. The living standard of lowest-rank foot soldiers was not much different from that of poor commoners. Among these samurai, those who did not have lords to serve were called *ronin*, or masterless samurai, and performed various kinds of jobs. Almost all samurai became literate, were engaged in administrative work, and maintained a high level of education.

In theory, the society was divided into four classes: samurai rulers, farmers, artisans, and merchants. The distinction between samurai and commoners was very strict, and intermarriage was forbidden. Commoners were not allowed to take family names and were identified by their given names and the name of the place where they lived. Among the commoners, farmers were placed on the top in theory; however, the farmers' life was hard. They were obliged to till the land and paid high rent (feudal tax) amounting to 40–60 percent of the yield. They inherited farmland through their own family, yet all the land was regarded as belonging to the feudal lord. The artisans and merchants, collectively identified as townsmen, were placed lowest in the social order; however, as the money economy developed, they prospered and created a rich bourgeois culture. Many elements of what we now call traditional culture were developed by the townsmen of the Tokugawa period: kabuki and *bunraku* (puppet) theaters, *haiku*, and banquets with entertainment by courtesans (*geisha*).

For over 260 years under Tokugawa rule, Japan secluded itself from the outside world. Foreign trade was restricted to the port of Nagasaki, with the exception of controlled trade through the island of Tsushima and the kingdom of Ryukyu (Okinawa). In Nagasaki, only the Chinese and Dutch traders were allowed to stay in designated areas. Dutch doctors and scholars who accompanied the traders were the only source of information about the Western countries and Western science and technology. Overseas travel by the Japanese was strictly banned, and Christianity was severely proscribed because it was regarded as subversive. Under this rigid control, peace and stability brought prosperity to Tokugawa Japan. Its population increased from around 20 million to 30 million and remained stable at that level.

Japan as a Modern Nation State

The Meiji Restoration

In the nineteenth century, the Western nations desired to expand their trade with Asia and pressured Japan to open its doors. In 1853 the United States dispatched navy ships under the command of Commodore Matthew C. Perry, who signed the first United States–Japan Friendship Treaty. Later in 1858 the Tokugawa bakufu signed comprehensive trade agreements with the United States and major European powers. These treaties were unequal in that they gave the foreigners extraterritorial privileges to live in Japan under the protection of their own laws, and to limit Japan's ability to determine import taxes on foreign goods.

The bakufu's handling of foreign relations triggered an anti-Tokugawa movement, which was spearheaded by junior samurai from several domains. As the entire country fell into turmoil, heated debate took place. The core of the issue was how to deal with the national crisis caused by the foreign threat. Ultimately the allied forces of Satsuma and Choshu (the largest domains in southern Kyushu and western Honshu) along with some other allied domains seized control of the imperial court, and in the name of the emperor they announced on January 3, 1868, restoration of direct rule by the emperor. Without great resistance, the last shogun of the Tokugawa bakufu resigned by returning his title to the emperor. The emperor moved to Edo, which was renamed Tokyo (Eastern Capital). Ever since, the Tokugawa shogun's castle has been used as the imperial palace. Before long, all the feudal lords returned their fiefs to the emperor and retired with generous pensions. This entire development is known as the Meiji Restoration. Meiji (bright rule) was the period name of this emperor's reign (1868–1912). It was followed by Taisho (1912–1926), Showa (1926–1989) and Heisei (1989–   ).

The Development of Modern Japan (1868–1945)

The leaders of the newly created government ruled Japan under the name of the emperor, who was 16 years old at the time of the Restoration. They were the samurai-administrators mainly of Satsuma and Choshu who had led the anti-Tokugawa movement. They carried out policies for sweeping reform to build a modern state, developed its economy through industrialization, built up strong military forces by adopting modern technology and organization, and endeavored to catch up with the West in all aspects of modern civilization.

Under this new regime, feudal status and the privileges of the samurai class were abolished and all people were declared equal. A universal system of education was created under which all boys and girls would receive at least primary education. Universal military conscription was installed, making military service (which formerly was the privilege of samurai) the duty of all people. Farmers' ownership rights of land were confirmed, and the freedom to sell and purchase lands was established. A fixed tax on land was the major source of revenue for the new regime in the early years.

To modernize the economy, a national currency was established with the *yen* as its unit and a modern banking system was created. Infrastructures necessary for industrialization such as telegraph systems, railroads, and lighthouses were built. The government built factories for military uniforms, weapons and ammunition, bricks for Western-style buildings, and other commodities that were not traditionally used. As pilot projects for modernization, the government started plants in various other areas. To improve the quality of silk, tea, and other export commodities, it sponsored trade fairs. At great expense, it hired foreign experts in various fields as technicians, advisors, and teachers. Selected students were sent abroad to study in Germany, Britain, France, and the United States, and on their return they were given responsible positions.

Not only for the sake of modernization but also for the purpose of promoting the newly international status of Japan, the Meiji government instituted modern political systems. The most important national goal of Japan was to establish its equal place in the modern international community. This goal was fully achieved only after World War II. The immediate goal of the Meiji generation was to revise the unequal treaties by abolishing extraterritoriality and gaining autonomy in deciding customs duties. In order to be recognized as a country deserving of equal treatment by the Western powers, Japan had to prove that its legal and political systems were modernized. Under the constitution promulgated in 1889, the Diet (parliament) system was created, and the first national election for the House of Representatives took place in the following year. Despite being very limited, it was the beginning of the democratic system of government, and in 1925 all adult men gained voting rights.

During the Meiji era Japan fought two major wars against China and Russia. Although they were relatively weak at the time, these countries were great empires, and Japan's victory over them surprised the world. The first war was in 1894–1895 against China over control of Korea, which was thereafter declared an independent state. This opened the way for Japan to increase its influence over Korea and eventually to annex it as part of the Japanese empire in 1910. Under the peace treaty at the end of the war with China in 1895, Japan acquired Taiwan from China and ruled the island as a colony until the end of World War II. Under the treaty Japan also gained the southern peninsula of Manchuria from China; however, Russia forced Japan to give it up with threat of joint action by Russia, Germany, and France. To build greater military and economic strength, Japan made concentrated efforts for the next decade and was victorious in the 1904–1905 war against Russia. As a result, Japan acquired rights to build and defend its railway system in southern Manchuria, and it gained territory on the southern half of Sakhalin island (north of Hokkaido).

Around the time of World War I, Japan's economy prospered and trends toward democracy advanced as voting rights were expanded. Political parties developed, and the prime minister, who was formerly nominated from among the oligarchs, was chosen from among the leaders of political parties. However, this trend was blocked in the 1930s when military leaders gained control of the government. Despite industrial growth, large segments of the population were left behind in terms of modern development; in particular, tenant farmers in rural areas experienced serious economic problems. Uneven development resulting from hasty industrialization caused great dissatisfaction and distrust in parliamentary politics.

When Japan's international trade contracted following the outbreak of a worldwide economic depression in 1929, Japan's anxiety over supplies of natural resources for its domestic industry intensified. A majority of Japanese thought that the creation of a self-sufficient economic zone was the only way to achieve national survival. When the military took its own actions in Manchuria and put that area under its control in 1931, the government in Tokyo accepted this move and supported the puppet state of Manchukuo established by the military. Then the Japanese government extended its control beyond Manchuria into northern China. Soon thereafter Chinese resistance against the Japanese invasion, followed by Japanese military suppression of the resistance, developed into full-scale war in 1937.

The United States was strongly opposed to the Japanese expansion into China and other areas of East Asia. After World War II broke out and France fell to the Nazis, Japan occupied North Vietnam in 1940 and South Vietnam in the following summer. The United States tightened its economic sanctions against Japan and in the summer of 1941 put a ban on the shipment of oil, which was essential for the Japanese to continue the war in China. The military leaders of Japan found it unthinkable to follow the American demand to withdraw from China, including Manchuria, which most of the Japanese regarded as essential for their economic survival. Japan continued diplomatic negotiations to obtain a compromise from the United States on Japan's interests in the Chinese continent; however, the failure of diplomatic efforts became increasingly clear. Then the military leadership under General TOJO Hideki decided to seize Indonesian oil and, for the purpose of neutralizing the American navy until Japan could establish its control in Southeast Asia, bombed Pearl Harbor on December 7, 1941.

The war in the Pacific was catastrophic for the Japanese people as well as for the Chinese and other Asians who suffered great atrocities inflicted by the Japanese military. The people in Japan were mobilized to continue the war efforts under extreme deprivation, and the military leaders insisted on fighting to the last soldier. As the supply of oil and ammunition dwindled toward the end of the war, *kamikaze* fighters flew with only enough fuel for a one-way trip toward enemy ships or airplanes, crashing into them as human bombs.

It was only after the Americans dropped atomic bombs on Hiroshima and Nagasaki, and the Soviet Union declared war on Japan in August 1945, that the Japanese government decided to surrender to the Allied Powers. On August 15 the emperor's statement telling the people that Japan must "bear the unbearable" was broadcast over the radio. It was the first time that the Japanese people had ever heard the voice of their emperor. In postwar Japan the myth of divine origin of the imperial family was thoroughly denied, and the emperor was presented as a human being.

When the war ended, Japanese people were exhausted and demoralized. For over five decades to this day, antiwar sentiment has been the deepest national sentiment. A strong consensus has been against the use of nuclear weapons by any country.

The New Japan after World War II (1945–Present)

Under the military occupation by the Allied Powers led by General Douglas MacArthur, Japan experienced reforms on a scale comparable to that of the restructuring after the Meiji Restoration. The primary goal of the Allied Powers was to demilitarize Japan and deprive it of the economic and political ability to rebuild its military forces. By the time the occupation ended in 1952, however, the Cold War had forced the United States to shift its emphasis toward reviving Japan's industrial sector.

The New Constitution drafted by MacArthur's staff as an amendment to the 1889 Constitution came into effect in 1947. It defined the emperor as a symbol of the state without political power, made clear that the prime minister must be elected via majority votes in the Diet, and required that members of both Houses of the Diet be chosen by national election. People's rights were expanded, including equality between the sexes. There was a saying in the postwar era that "stockings and women became stronger in Japan after the war." Indeed, nylon stockings and women's voting rights symbolized the progress of postwar Japan in economic and political freedom.

As to the military forces, the New Constitution specifically forbade the maintenance of any war potential and renounced war forever. The Japanese people, who had felt betrayed by their military leaders, enthusiastically welcomed this. Renunciation of war is still a basic principle of Japan's international relations.

The thoroughgoing land reform during the occupation allowed tenant farmers to become owners of the land they tilled. When the national economy improved and the green revolution caused farmers to become more productive and prosperous, they provided a market for industrial goods. Rural districts were important power bases of the Liberal Democratic Party, which shaped the post-occupation economic policies for half a century.

To facilitate free competition and democratization in the economy, the occupation reform dissolved huge business conglomerates, known as *zaibatsu*, which had been formed around the families of Mitsui, Mitsubishi, Sumitomo, and the like. Moreover, executive officers of large companies were purged, enabling junior managers to take over leadership positions that allowed them innovative business management. To help rebuild Japan's economy, Americans generously extended financial and technological aid. The transfer of new technology was easy because most of the old infrastructure of Japan had been destroyed in the war. The Japanese people who had been nurtured in the traditional ethic of diligence and believed in the virtue of thriftiness had saved a good portion of their income, thereby providing capital for economic development. The system of lifetime employment generated workers' dedication to their companies and kept their morale high. To promote an export economy, Japan's currency exchange rate was fixed at 360 yen to one U.S. dollar; this remained unchanged until 1971, when a floating exchange rate was introduced. These factors and the international environment contributed to Japan's unprecedented economic growth following the occupation.

In education, the European-style two-tiered system for the elite and non-elite was replaced with the American system. Compulsory education was expanded to the ninth grade, and coeducation became the norm. To accommodate greater numbers of students, many new national universities were created all over the country. After the rapid economic growth of the 1960s, many private colleges and universities were created, and almost half the nation's young people received a college education.

By the end of the twentieth century, Japan has become a world economic power. During the past half-century since the end of the Pacific War, the primary focus of national efforts has been economic development. The Japanese people have cooperated with the system that operates on a close alliance among big business, bureaucracy, and the Liberal Democratic Party. Men work hard for long hours, causing family life to take second place. Most women accept their positions as homemakers and assistance to men at work. Japan's international environment under the protection of the United States during the Cold War benefited its development a great deal. In return for American military protection, it provided military bases to the United States. In following the American policy to contain Communist China, Japan maintained only a limited unofficial relationship with mainland China until the United States announced a change in its China policy in 1971. The collapse of the Soviet Union and the end of the Cold War in the late 1980s changed the fundamental framework in which Japan maintained its prosperity.

The Japanese political and economic systems that made Japan an advanced industrial power during the Cold War era have been going through gradual but fundamental changes. This was symbolized in the early 1990s by the fact that the ruling conservative party lost the majority seats in the Diet. In the late 1990s, Japan's transformation is not the result of purposeful reforms but a necessary adjustment to the post–Cold War world.

NOTES

1. The foundation of Japanese identity provided in mythological accounts was used as the basis of history textbooks for all levels of education in modern Japan until the end of the Pacific War.

2. Robert Borgen and Marian Ury, "Readable Japanese Mythology: Selections from *Nihon shoki* and *Kojiki*," *Journal of Teachers of Japanese* 24, no. 1 (1990).

3. In those early years, there were several women emperors in Japan. Today, however, the law concerning the Imperial Household stipulates that only male members of the imperial family are qualified to succeed the emperor.

4. The reign title was a Chinese tradition. The emperor named all or a part of his reign to reflect his wishes for that period. The tradition of reign title was adopted by the Japanese starting in 645. Just as in China, one emperor could change the reign title as many times as he wished while he was on the throne. Since 1868, however, one reign title has been used for the entire period of each emperor's reign. "Heisei" is the reign title of the current emperor, who was enthroned in 1989. The date in official documents in Japan today is written with the reign title, and 1998 is recorded as the tenth year of Heisei.

2

Thought and Religion

THE INFLUENCE OF CONFUCIANISM

In shaping Japanese thinking beyond primitive animism, Confucianism had a profound influence throughout the nation's history. "Confucianism" is the Western name given to the Chinese philosophy developed on the teachings of an ancient teacher, Confucius (the Latinized name given to Kong Qiu, 551–479 B.C.). In China, this philosophy provided the basic principles of moral conduct, family ethics, social relations, and government. The central concepts of the Confucian ethic were summarized in the Three Cardinal Relationships, namely, the relationships between father and son, ruler and subjects, husband and wife. Son's filial piety to father, people's loyalty and obedience to the ruler, and wife's faithfulness to husband were regarded as the basic norms, which could be applied to other relationships in society as well. In this teaching, emphasis is on the obligation of the inferior to the superior. The assumption is that society needs a hierarchical order in which every individual has his or her own place, and that peace and harmony prevail if everyone follows the proper manner of conduct. These concepts were well suited to Japanese society, especially during the Tokugawa regime from the early seventeenth through the mid-nineteenth century. At that time, Confucianism formed the core curriculum in schools for the ruling elite and commoners.

Confucian teachings emphasized uprightness, righteousness, loyalty, sincerity, reciprocity, and benevolence as personal virtues. These principles were readily accepted by the Japanese, whose concept of *makoto* (truthfulness, pure-heartedness, honesty) emphasizes sincerity. The principle of filial piety was useful during the Tokugawa period when family was the social and economic unit of society. Occupation and property belonged to the family rather than to the individual. For every family of samurai, farmer, craftsman, or merchant, continuation of the family line was a foremost concern because it was the premise for keeping one's position and salary (samurai), farmland (farmer), or business (craftsman or merchant). Individuals often sacrificed their happiness to ensure survival of the family. Filial love toward parents was the central principle of family relations, and it was extended to the long-deceased ancestors to whom the family owed its status and property.

The Confucian concepts of hierarchy in human society and respect for age were useful in the feudal society under Tokugawa rule that was structured hierarchically. Its stability rested on individuals' dutiful fulfillment of obligations to their superiors and maintenance of proper conduct in daily life. The general rules of conduct were respect for seniors in social rank and age, and acknowledgment of the superiority of man over woman. After Japan was centralized under the Meiji government in the nineteenth century, the concept of filial piety was expanded to embrace the idea of loyalty to the emperor, who was regarded as father of the entire nation. Moral education in elementary schools inculcated loyalty to the state as well as filial piety, diligence, and self-discipline. After the war, moral education in schools was abolished and the emperor-centered view of history was denounced.

Time-honored concepts do not easily change. Although the Japanese today, especially the younger generation, are much more individualistic and independent-minded than prewar generations, they still emphasize the importance of group harmony and are willing to follow others rather than take independent action based on individual judgment and initiative. In today's Japan, seniority by age is still respected. Promotion in most public and private organizations is based on the length of service, which is usually geared to the age of the individuals. Reciprocity is emphasized in social relations. Individuals do their best to reciprocate a favor received in order to maintain a long-lasting relationship. This concept underlies the custom of seasonal gift-giving for maintenance of social ties.

Education is the key to success in modern Japan, just as in the United States. Because academic degrees are important, competition for acceptance at prestigious schools is intense. At the same time, learning is valued for its own sake. In fact, love of learning was one of the Confucian traits. Common people in Japan have faith in life-long learning for the sake of personal improvement. It is assumed that educated people are morally superior. In

Confucian tradition, brilliant but evil scientists like the fictional Dr. Frankenstein did not appear.

It has been often said that the Confucian ethic of diligence, self-discipline, frugality, loyalty, and dedication to the family enhanced the performance of Japanese workers and facilitated Japan's progress toward becoming a highly industrialized nation. Some observers even argue that the Confucian ethic was essential for the modernization of East Asia, just as the Protestant ethic was for Europe. It goes without saying that these moral values are important for a successful society; however, they are not exclusive to Confucianism or even necessarily derived from it. Nevertheless, the norms and ethic of pre-industrial societies in China and Japan that contributed to their subsequent stability and prosperity are often labeled as Confucian.

RELIGION

For most Japanese today, formal religion involves rites and services more than religious doctrines or discipline. Yet people regard religious sentiment as important. In surveys conducted during the 1980s and 1990s, when asked whether they have any religious belief, about 30 percent of the Japanese people admitted that they do. To the question "Do you believe in the existence of *kami* (Shinto deity) or *hotoke* (Buddha)?" over 50 percent said "yes," and about 80 percent said that religious spirit is important.

Most Japanese accept Shinto and Buddhism simultaneously. Typically, Japanese marry before a Shinto altar and are buried, after cremation, in a Buddhist funeral. Many people, young and old, pay a New Years visit to a Shinto shrine and visit family graves once or twice a year. Young couples take their children to a Shinto shrine at the *shichi-go-san* festival to celebrate the ages 3, 5, and 7. For funeral and periodic memorial services, a family invites a priest from a Buddhist temple that belongs to the same Buddhist sect with which the family ancestors were affiliated. In the past, every family in Japan had to be registered at a Buddhist temple to comply with the anti-Christian policy of the Tokugawa government (1600–1868). After the country was opened to the Western world in the mid-nineteenth century, the Christian faith and ethic attracted many influential leaders among intellectuals; however, the number of Christians in Japan has remained only 1 or 2 percent of the entire population.

In addition to shrines, temples, and churches affiliated with traditional Shinto, Buddhism, and Christianity, there are numerous organizations that espouse new religions. Even though their followers are not numerous (about

Altar of a Tenrikyo church. Courtesy of Noriko Kamachi.

3% of the population), some have exerted significant political influence be-cause of their strong organization or have attracted attention because of their aggressiveness. Among the "new religions," Tenrikyo, Konkokyo, Omotokyo (-kyo means "religious teaching"), and others that were founded in the late nineteenth century, mostly as offshoots of Shinto, are the oldest. Soka Gakkai (Value Creating Society) and Reiyukai (Society of Companions of the Spirits), Buddhist offshoots, and PL Kyodan (Church of Perfect Liberty) are prominent examples of new religions that developed following World War II. After around 1975, new types of religious cults proliferated. Unlike the followers of the previously established new religions who sought release from illness, poverty, or conflicts and hoped to gain worldly benefits, adherents to the most recent cults, such as Aum Shinrikyo (Aum Supreme Truth), are younger people who are drawn to the cult leaders' promise to help their followers develop supernormal creative powers.

Shinto

The indigenous religion of Japan is called Shinto, which literally means "the way of *kami*" (the superior being). *Kami* can be interpreted as gods, deities, or extraordinary spirits. Shinto stemmed from animistic beliefs in ancient times. In the minds of ancient people, everything in nature—including mountains, rivers, trees, and plants—as well as every living creature, had a spirit. In their view, nature was permeated with all sorts of spirits. People venerated extraordinary things such as sublime mountains, giant trees, unusual boulders, and natural phenomena such as waterfalls, lightning, storms, and so on, because they appeared to be the manifestation of powerful spirits.

Despite the fact that Japan experienced natural calamities caused by typhoons and earthquakes, people had optimistic views of nature and were thankful for the mild climate and the predictable transition of the four seasons. They believed that there was inherent harmony in pristine nature and feared to disturb it by causing *kegare* (defilement or pollution). Sin (*tsumi*) essentially was offense against others or violation of social norms, and it was regarded to result from the pollution of the offender's mind. In their views, the human world and the natural world were interrelated; therefore disruption of social order was an offense against cosmic order, which could cause disaster. In order to prevent calamity, the offense had to be neutralized by purification.

Shinto stressed the importance of purity, sincerity, and harmony but did not develop clearly defined doctrines. As for the writings of Shinto theology, there are only fragmentary expressions in the earliest chronicles (*Kojiki* and *Nihon shoki*) and in the prayers recorded in a tenth-century compendium of rituals, *Engishiki*.

Shinto developed a complex of rituals that centered on chanting of prayer (*norito*) and ritual purification, either by ritual dusters or by cleansing in water. Even in modern times, the purification rite is important for the Japanese. It is customary to sprinkle a pinch of salt on a person who comes back from a funeral to cleanse death pollution before the person enters the house. When constructing a new building, people purify the ground. Even abroad, when a Japanese automobile assembly plant was built in Michigan in the 1980s, Shinto priests were flown in from California for the ground-breaking ceremony.[1] At the inauguration of a FSX fighter built with help from American companies in the 1990s, Shinto priests performed an elaborate purification rite, chanting *norito* and waving sacred branches in front of the fighter plane.[2]

During the Yayoi and Tomb periods, primitive villages in Japan developed into regional communities under the leadership of powerful clans. The leaders of the clans who strove to expand their territories claimed not only political authority but also religious authority attached to the worship of the region's guardian deities. These deities were regarded to be the ancestors of the leading clan, and the clan chief monopolized the ritual authority to worship the deities.

The Sun Goddess (Amaterasu) was the ancestor deity of the clan who founded the imperial rule in Yamato Plain, known as the Yamato Court. Being the ancestor of the imperial clan, Amaterasu was promoted to the highest seat in the Shinto pantheon. To this day, her shrine in Ise has been maintained by the imperial household. The emperor and members of the imperial family visit this shrine to report their coming of age, marriage, and succession to the throne. The most important ritual in imperial succession is *Daijosai* (great feast of enthronement), in which the new emperor shares a meal with his ancestral deities in a sacred hall in the palace compound.

Other ancient clans maintained shrines for their ancestral deities in the provinces. Among them, Izumo Shrine on the coast of the Japan Sea is the most prominent. It enshrines the ancestor deities of the powerful clan in Izumo who contested the hegemony of the Yamato Court to the final stage of the struggle for national unification.

When Japan began to build a modern nation state in the mid-nineteenth century, the leadership of the new government used Shinto as a state ideology and promoted emperor worship as the spiritual core of patriotism. The myth of the divine origin of the imperial family was declared in the constitution of 1889 and was written in school textbooks as historical fact. Until the end of World War II in the Pacific in 1945, Shinto shrines were placed under state patronage and control. At every school auditorium an altar for the "sacred image" of the emperor was built, and students and teachers were made to listen to the recitation of the Imperial Edicts on Education at every important ceremony. After the war, the principle of the separation of state and religion was stipulated in the New Constitution of 1947.

Shinto shrines were often built near rivers, lakes, or seashores with scenic beauty, if not on top of a mountain. However, not all shrines are dedicated to nature gods. An unattended shrine surrounded with woods in the middle of rice paddies is typically a shrine of the ancestral deity (*ujigami*) of a village community. Presumably, the ancestral deity of a powerful clan was accepted by villagers as their common ancestor. Villagers take their newborns to the shrine to ask for divine protection. They use the shrine building and the surrounding ground for communal activities, such as the thanksgiving festival after harvest. Whether or not one partakes in communal activities centered around the shrine, everyone in the village is regarded as a parishioner. By the same token, town dwellers are regarded as parishioners of a shrine in the neighborhood, whether or not they give any shrine parishioners' contribu-

Torii (sacred arch) at the entrance to a Shinto shrine. Courtesy of Noriko Kamachi.

tion. In this way, all Japanese are assumed to be parishioners of the Shinto religion.

Some city shrines are dedicated to the spirit of prominent individuals of the past. For example, there are shrines all over Japan for SUGAWARA Michizane (later known as Tenjin), a learned minister of the ninth century. These shrines are popular among students who wish to get his help to pass entrance examinations for colleges. Some shrines are dedicated to a group of people. In Tokyo, there is a shrine dedicated to the souls of the soldiers who died in wars.

The buildings of most Shinto shrines are simple and similar, in principle, to the shrine in Ise dedicated to the legendary ancestors of the imperial family. Usually the shrines are made of unpainted wood and covered with thatched roofs with crossbeams. Major shrines are rebuilt at regular intervals of twenty or thirty years. In Ise the building dedicated to Amaterasu is destroyed every twenty years, and a new one is built in facsimile at the alternate lot adjacent to it.

At the entrance to a shrine, a sacred arch (*torii*), made either of wood or stone, stands as a distinct landmark of a Shinto shrine. Between the sacred arch and the main hall there is a water fountain for visitors to cleanse their hands and rinse their mouths before worshipping. At the entrance of the shrine building, visitors may sound the large bell hanging from the beam by shaking the long rope attached to it. In the altar inside the building, a sacred object is kept. It may be a portrait of the individual who is enshrined, a mirror, or a piece of gem, rock, or wood, which is supposed to represent the god. Whatever it may be, worshippers do not see it and are not much concerned about it. Ordinary worshippers are not allowed to enter the shrine building. They stand at the entrance, bow to the altar, throw money into the offering box, clap their hands twice to summon the god's attention, press their palms together with their eyes closed, and offer prayer in silence. Then they bow once more and leave.

As a sideline service, large shrines offer oracles that are printed on small pieces of paper. Worshippers who draw a sacred lot (*o-mikuji*) and receive an oracle may tie it to the branch of a tree there if they do not want to accept it. Worshippers may buy a votive plaque, a postcard-size wooden plate called *ema* (literally, "picture horse"), write their pleas and wishes on it, and hang it in a space provided for the purpose. The wishes are supposed to be delivered by the horse drawn on the plaque. Nowadays, the pictures on the plaques are not limited to horses; they symbolize various kinds of good luck or common wishes of the worshippers. They are mostly wishes for good health, family harmony, good luck in college entrance exams, or success in business.

During the festivals of large urban shrines, a portable shrine (*o-mikoshi*) is carried out in a procession by a crowd of parishioners. The procession makes a round to extend the benefit of the divine benefit and, at the same time, collect alms. Supposedly, the course of the portable shrine is directed by the god inside it.

Buddhism

Buddhism, which originated in India as a teaching of the Buddha (Enlightened One), was transmitted to Japan through China and Korea sometime in the mid-sixth century and exerted profound influence on Japanese culture. For acceptance of Buddhism by Japan's ruling elite, the role of Prince Shotoku (547–622) was instrumental. He served the Suiko emperor (one of several women emperors in Japanese history) as her regent and had great influence in the Yamato Court. Horyuji temple, the world's oldest surviving wooden structure, was built by his order. Part of Buddhism's appeal to the rulers of ancient states was the belief that worshipping Buddha, promoting his teaching, and supporting the monastic community would protect the state from external threat. During the Nara period, Buddhist temples and monasteries were accorded state patronage, and the clergy enjoyed high pres-

Gate at a Buddhist temple. Courtesy of Noriko Kamachi.

tige and influence. The mainstream of Nara Buddhism was represented by the six major sects of Mahayana Buddhism, which focused on scholarly discourse of doctrines.

Buddhism brought Japan not only new religious thought and ritual but also a new style of building, sculpture, painting, and liturgical music. It also served as a vehicle for the transmission of the writing system developed in China. Buddhist scriptures and Confucian classics were the earliest Chinese texts brought to Japan at a time when the Japanese did not have their own writing system. The Japanese adopted the Chinese writing system and later created their own syllabary for additional use.

The teaching of Buddha was rooted in the ancient Indian conception of life, death, and afterlife as represented in the cycle of birth, death, and rebirth. To be reborn as a human being, animal, insect, or hungry ghost is determined by *karma* (the cause and the result). In this belief, every intentional act has a result that will produce an effect in the future life. Rebirth as a human, regarded to be the result of a virtuous deed, is considered very rare. Indian philosophy also has an elaborate cosmology built on a belief that there are three realms of the universe. "The realm of desire" is the place where all living creatures and hungry ghosts live. Various kinds of hells are extensions of this realm. Above it, there are "the realm of form" and "the formless realm" where grand bliss prevails; these realms are inhabited by gods.

According to a long-accepted tradition, the Buddha (also referred to as Shakyamuni, 563–483 B.C.) was born as a prince, named Siddhartha, in a kingdom in what is today Nepal. Even though he was surrounded by nothing but beauty and pleasures in his palace, his mind was torn by existential questions. Finally at the age of 29 he followed a religious mendicant, leaving his wife and an infant son behind, and sought liberation from the endless sufferings caused by the cycle of deaths and rebirths. After many years of ascetic practices for religious training, he led a life of meditation in a forest and finally came to an enlightenment that made him the Buddha (Enlightened One), forever free of future rebirth. When he emerged from the forest he gave his first teaching, which is known as the "four noble truths."

The first truth is that life is inevitable suffering inherent in birth, aging, sickness, and death. The second truth is that the cause of suffering is negative *karma* resulting from negative mental states such as desire and hatred. The third truth is that if one could destroy the negative mental states such as desire and hatred, one could cease suffering. The fourth truth is the path (technique) to end the negative mental states: it is through ethic (conscious restraint of nonvirtuous deeds), meditation (sufficient level of concentration), and wisdom (insight or enlightenment). One who can end the negative mental state and achieve enlightenment can be liberated from the cycle of birth and rebirth and can pass into *nirvana* (the state of bliss).

Early followers of the Buddha led monastic lives that required poverty (nonpossession of property), celibacy, and inoffensiveness (not taking life from any living creature). Their Buddhism was called Theravada (Elders' Teaching), or Hinayana (Small Vehicle) by those who started another tradition a few centuries later. In this new tradition, Mahayana (Great Vehicle), lay people can attain enlightenment by faith only, because Boddhisattva (Enlightened One), who was qualified to pass into nirvana, stayed in this world out of compassion to help others achieve salvation.

It was the Mahayana school of Buddhism that was transmitted to China, Korea, and then Japan. Within this school, various sects were developed by those who studied different sutras (i.e., written texts of Buddha's teaching), and followed different interpretations of the Buddha's teaching.

During the Nara period, the six sects of Mahayana Buddhism retained the highly scholastic tradition of India. During the Heian period and thereafter, new sects of Buddhism incorporated the animistic view of the universe indigenous to Japan. In the process of Japanization of Buddhism, Saicho and Kukai, who founded the Tendai and Shingon sects respectively, stand out as the most creative figures. Saicho held that all human beings had buddha-nature and therefore could achieve buddhahood. Kukai believed that buddha-nature was not limited to human beings and was immanent in all living creatures. This belief is similar to the indigenous Japanese belief that everything in nature has spirit.

Also during the Heian period, an eclectic interpretation of the relationship between Shinto and Buddhism developed. In this view the Buddha represented a universal truth and *kami* was a local incarnation of Buddha.

From around the tenth century, there was an upheaval of faith in Pure Land or Western Paradise of Amida Buddha. This faith spread widely—first in aristocratic circles in Kyoto and then among the common people—by the evangelical activities of Honen (1133–1212), Shinran (1173–1263), and Nichiren (1222–1282), who founded Jodoshu (Pure Land sect), Jodo shinshu (New Pure Land sect), and Nichirenshu (Japanese Lotus sect), respectively. They denied one's own power to attain salvation and emphasized the importance of realizing human imperfection. In their teaching, salvation comes only by throwing oneself upon the mercy of Amida Buddha by chanting the name of Amida in undivided devotion. The phrase for chanting, *Namu Amida Butsu* (*Nammaida* in short form), meant "I rely upon Amida Buddha." In Nichiren sect, the phrase is *Namu Myo Horengekyo* (*Nammyo Horengekyo* in short form), meaning "I rely upon the wondrous Lotus Sutra." Since these new sects did not require scholarly discourse or disciplined meditation, they appealed to the common people and attracted a large number of followers.

The Zen sect is centered on meditation, the disciplined concentration of mind. It spread among the warriors during the Kamakura period and was patronized by the Kamakura and Muromachi shogunates. Founders of the oldest Zen monasteries in Japan were Eisai (1141–1215) and Dogen (1200–1253), both of whom studied in Zen monasteries in China. Along with Zen Buddhism they brought to Japan the Chinese custom of tea drinking in monasteries, following which a Zen culture evolved that valued quiet simplicity and aesthetic appreciation of nature. Zen culture had an overwhelming impact on the arts and architecture of Japan. It inspired a new style of calligraphy, painting, flower arrangement, "studio-style" house, landscape garden, *noh* drama, and literature. Visitors to Kamakura can see the buildings of Kenchoji, Engakuji, and other monasteries built during the Kamakura period. They testify to the austere life of the monks who concentrated on Zen questions while sitting in meditation and during physical labor.

In Kyoto, there are elegant compounds of Zen monasteries such as Nanzenji and Daitokuji. These retreats enjoyed the patronage of the Muromachi shogunate and functioned as refined salons for the aristocratic elite. The famous rock garden of Ryoanji, the Golden Pavilion of Rokuonji, and the Silver Pavilion of Jishoji are examples of the world-renowned legacies of Zen culture. At the same time, however, intellectual passion and religious fervor ebbed in Zen monasteries. During the Warring States period, when secular power holders contested for hegemony, Buddhist communities were suppressed as obstacles to their political ambitions. As a result, monasteries lost their financial power and political influence.

The Tokugawa shogunate, which was founded in Edo (present-day Tokyo) in 1603, required every family in Japan to register at a Buddhist temple. This policy was an effort to stamp out Christianity, which spread during the Warring States period. Because of this policy, Buddhist temples became a familiar scene in every community. Since all the people were forced to become supporters of Buddhist temples, there was no need for Buddhists to make efforts to appeal to the minds and hearts of the people. It made the Buddhist clergy lose their passion for scholastic discourse on doctrine or rigorous standards of discipline. In modern Japan, monks are free to eat meat, marry, and raise families. At most temples the position of the resident priest is inherited in the same family. As a religious corporation, a typical Buddhist temple in modern Japan is not much more than a family business specializing in funeral and memorial services.

RELIGION IN DAILY LIFE

Household Religion

Because of the religious policy of the Tokugawa shogunate as discussed in the previous section, all Japanese today are Buddhist by default except for those who have converted to Christianity or one of the new religions. Everyone during the Tokugawa era was a parishioner of one of the Buddhist temples, and their descendants were regarded as parishioners of the same temple. Today, just about every family has an ancestral altar (butsudan) in the house. It is made in the same size and fashion as a cupboard, and some are small enough to be placed on top of a cupboard. They are painted with black lacquer, and some are decorated with gold.

Pious people offer prayer at the ancestral altar every day, burning incense and lighting candles. Some people make an offering of hot steamed rice in a small bowl as a routine ritual at each family meal. During the mid-summer Bon festival when the souls of the deceased are believed to come home for a three-day visit, many families—especially those who have lost family mem-

Family tomb. Courtesy of Kyodo News.

bers within the past year—hang paper lanterns around the house. They invite Buddhist priests for sutra chanting and make special offerings following a vegetarian menu. Most people, however, have little contact with Buddhist temples or priests except when they need to get help for funeral services.

Most families have a separate altar for the Shinto deity (*kamidana*) in their house. Ordinarily it is a tray-size shelf fixed on the beam in a corner of a room. Enshrined there is a talisman of a Shinto shrine printed on a sheet of white paper and wrapped in an envelope. Unglazed pottery cups for offering of *sake* (rice wine) or water and a pair of vases for sacred branches are placed on the shelf. Normally people don't pay attention to this shelf except for cleaning it at the end of the year and placing New Years decorations on it.

In and around old farmhouses in the countryside, many more altars and tiny shrines are built for various deities and spirits, such as the fox spirit (*inari*) and stove god (*kojin*). They too get decorations and offerings at New Years.

Rituals for the Dead

A funeral is a rite for sending the deceased to the other world. In the minds of the ancient Japanese, the other world was continuous with this world. The same sentiment lingers deep in the minds of modern people. They feel that the dead can see the activities in this world, just as those who are in the shade can see those who are in the light. When their beloved one dies, people take comfort in a belief that the dead watch over them from the other world. The duty of the living is to perform rituals for the dead and to fulfill the wishes of the dead, especially wishes for the well-being of family members.

Funeral customs vary from place to place, especially between the countryside and large cities. Nevertheless, there are many common elements in funerals throughout Japan. First, most funerals are given by the family of the dead at their own home. Funerals for important public figures take place at Buddhist temples or funeral halls that can accommodate large numbers of participants. Commercial funeral parlors for ordinary families are a rather new feature in Japan. Funeral companies help the families conduct funerals at home by sending equipment and personnel. The level of formalities and elaboration of ritual vary from family to family. The following is an outline of traditional practices among ordinary people.

When the death of the person appears imminent, each of the family members assemble at the bedside. They take turns wetting the dying person's lips with a brush dipped in water. This ritual is known as giving the last earthly water. It is said to be a desperate effort to bring back the soul that is about to depart from the mouth. Despite such an effort, the dying takes the last breath. Then the relatives cling to the body and cry out, calling the name of the dead. They also call the name of the dead toward the rooftop, mountains surrounding the house, ocean, or bottom of the well. This rite of "calling the soul" is an attempt to call back the soul that has already departed from the body. After a while, the family sends messengers out to announce the death to relatives, close friends, and the family temple. Two people are always sent on this mission. In its origin, the purpose of this mission was to search for the departed soul. It was feared that the strength of one person was not enough for the task. Also, there is a belief that at the moment of death the soul might appear to a person who is very close by.

The family members of the dead cook rice as the first activity after the death has occurred. They heap the rice in a bowl, stick one chopstick in its center, and offer it to the dead person on a table at the bedside. In some cases they place a knife on the chest of the dead person to protect it from evil spirits. After a while, relatives and neighbors come around with "incense money," a contribution to the funeral expenses. Cash is wrapped in a white paper or an envelope with a printed design in black or dark green, on which the bearer writes his or her family name. On the back of the wrapping, his or her address and the amount of the money enclosed may be written. The amount of the incense money is determined by one's relationship to the family. The amount must match the incense money received from the dead person's family in the past (adjusted for inflation). Such reciprocal obligations between households may go back many generations. It is therefore very important to keep accurate records of the incense money received from others.

As to the preparation of the body for the funeral, kinsmen and close neighbors first wash it with warm water. They pour cold water into a wooden tub first, and then pour hot water into it. This is the other way around from what people normally do, because it is said that everything in the world of the dead is the opposite of things in this world. If there is a paper screen around the deathbed, the screen is placed upside down when the person dies. After washing, they dress the dead person in either the formal *kimono* that he or she used to wear or a piece of white cotton robe, folding the left side of the kimono under the right side. This is the opposite of what the living do. If it is a man, they shave his face. For a woman, they put on light makeup. Then they place a shroud over the body and wait for a priest to come and chant a Buddhist scripture at the bedside before placing the body in a coffin. Since the dead person is supposed to depart for a journey to the other world, it is common to dress the body in the outfit of a pilgrim, putting on a shoulder bag in which several things are placed: change for ferry money to cross the river between this world and the other, a talisman of Amida Buddha, and something the dead person used to cherish. Preparation also involves placing on one hand a rosary, and on the other hand a long cane; on the feet, white cotton gaiters and straw sandals.

For the wake, kinsmen and neighbors come to the house and make preparations. Since the family members who lived with the dead person are not supposed to cook food, they leave the task of cooking and serving food to the people who come to help. The wake starts with the chanting of a sutra by the priest, followed by a vegetarian meal. This continues throughout the night, keeping the candle and incense burning at the temporary altar where the coffin is placed. After friends and neighbors leave, the closest relatives spend the rest of the night before the altar exchanging memories of the dead, singing old songs, and even dancing in reminiscence.

The funeral ceremony takes place in the house on the following day or a few days later. The task for setting up the funeral altar is left to the crew from the funeral service company. They shroud the house with black and white drapes and hang a sign on the front door to announce the mourning. The ceremony begins with the chanting of sutra by a priest (or priests) to give Buddhist instructions to the dead. By this, the dead person is supposedly enlightened and the attachment to this world is cut. At this point, a spirit tablet (*ihai*) made of plain wood on which a Buddhist name is written in black ink is validated as the representation of the dead person. The ceremony ends after eulogies, offering of incense by every attendant, and more chanting of sutras. Then the cover of the coffin is removed for the family members and other attendants to bid a last farewell, after which the cover is replaced and each family member ceremoniously hits the nail on the cover. The undertakers finalize the nailing of the coffin, making loud sounds. In moving the coffin from the house, the front door is avoided. Instead, it is carried out through one of the sliding doors around the veranda. When the coffin leaves the house, the rice bowl of the dead person crashes to the ground. This is believed to be a device not to let the departed soul wander back to the house. In most cases nowadays, the coffin is taken to a crematorium and the family waits while the cremation takes place. Then they collect the ashes in an urn to take home. When entering the house, they have to be cleansed of the death pollution by having salt sprinkled, by stepping on fresh ashes of wood or straw, or by chewing uncooked rice. They place the urn on the family altar until the end of the 49-day initial mourning period.

A dead soul is believed to be gradually purified by periodic memorial services offered by the descendants, and eventually it turns into an ancestral spirit. Following the funeral ceremony, memorial services take place at the family altar on every seventh day. The services on the first seventh day and the forty-ninth day are the most important. On the forty-ninth day, the family invites a priest for sutra chanting. Thereafter, burial of the ashes takes place at the family cemetery. One year later the family invites relatives and close friends to a memorial service either at home or at a Buddhist temple, where they serve a meal after the ceremony. Those who are invited come with cash offerings wrapped in white envelopes or send cash offerings by registered mail. Memorial services are supposed to be repeated on the third, seventh, thirteenth, and thirty-third year after the death, but not many families follow this anymore. At the thirty-third year, the ancestral spirit of the dead is assumed to have turned into a *kami* who no longer needs services or the ancestor tablet. Such old tablets are set on fire to avoid inadvertent desecration.

NOTES

1. "Groundbreaking, Japanese style: Flat Rock New 'Home of Mazda'," *Detroit Free Press*, May 30, 1985, pp. 1A, 17A.

2. "A New Warplane's Murky Horizon: Controversy and Costs Dog Plans for a Joint U.S.-Japan Jet Fighter," *New York Times*, January 13, 1995, pp. C1, C12.

3

Literature

Literature in printed form is an important part of Japanese culture today, although not as much as before the age of television. Because the Japanese emulated the Confucian culture of China during the formation of their state and government institutions, literature became an essential part of education, as it was in China. Today in any large city or small town in Japan, one finds bookstores with a large portion of floor space dedicated to literature. A typical small neighborhood bookstore carries copies of selected classical and contemporary literature. Even at tiny stalls on the platforms of train stations with barely enough room for one salesperson to sit inside, some pocket book editions of popular contemporary novels and essays are sold along with newspapers and weekly magazines. According to government statistics, more than one-quarter of the books published in Japan in the late 1980s were literary works.[1]

These works are published not only as books or in literary magazines but also in daily newspapers. Most papers have columns for *tanka* (short poems), shorter *haiku*, and *senryu* (satiric short poems) contributed by readers. Also, newspapers usually serialize one or two novels, some of which are later published as monographs. Certain best-sellers, such as novels by NATSUME Soseki in the early twentieth century and ARIYOSHI Sawako in the 1960s, were produced in this way.

Publishing of literary works is not limited to professional writers. At work places or in Japanese society at large, there are numerous circles and associations for *haiku, tanka, senryu,* and other genres. Many publish their own

Train on Sunday. Courtesy of Noriko Kamachi.

periodical magazines. Very often these kinds of groups are formed around an accomplished poet who serves as mentor for the group.

Literature in contemporary Japan is rooted in layers of legacies accumulated from the ancient past. In addition, it has absorbed many elements from modern European literature. Continuity in the Japanese literary tradition is very strong. The language used in the oldest books, namely, *Kojiki* (Records of Ancient Matters, A.D. 712) and *Nihon shoki* (Chronicles of Japan, A.D. 720), is not much different from the modern language. One does not need to be a specialist to read these oldest chronicles, as long as they are transcribed in modern script. Copies of these classics are in constant supply, both in annotated scholarly editions and paperback pocket book editions. For writers throughout the ages, classic literature has provided a source of inspiration and a reminder of the roots of commonly shared sentiments among the Japanese. For these reasons, one cannot fully understand modern Japanese literature without some knowledge of the literary legacies from its past.

TRADITIONAL LITERATURE

Waka (Japanese Poems)

Just as in other cultures, poetry is the oldest form of literature in Japan. It is regarded as the most sublime form of recording human feelings. The

Kiosk on train platform. Courtesy of Noriko Kamachi.

ceremony of poetry reading at the imperial palace is still an annual event during the New Years season. Every year the theme of the next year's poems is announced, and people are invited to send their contributions composed in the form of *tanka* (also called *waka*), which has long been the mainstay of traditional Japanese poetry. The authors of chosen poems are invited to a ceremony where the emperor and imperial family members present their own poems, which are recited by a professional reader. Chosen authors are from all walks of life, living not only in various areas of Japan but also in Hawaii, Brazil, and other parts of the world. This imperial tradition is a reflection of the ancient legacy of compiling an anthology of poems by the sovereign emperor, imperial family members, and his subjects—including aristocrats and commoners.

Kojiki, the earliest written history, is a repository of the earliest poems. Even poems by mythological heroes and heroines are recorded as part of the stories in it. Most of these are in combinations of five- and seven-syllable lines, which remain the basic rhythm of Japanese poetry.

The oldest anthology of poems, *Man'yoshu* (Ten Thousand Leaves, 20 vols.), was compiled during the second half of the eighth century and is regarded as the ultimate model of Japanese poetry. It contains 4,530 poems by emperors of earlier ages, imperial princes, princesses, noble men, noble women, government officials, monks, beggars, soldiers on frontier guard duty, peasants, and many unidentifiable poets who lived between the fourth century A.D. and the mid-eighth century. (The earliest identified composer of a poem was a legendary consort of the Nintoku emperor [A.D. 313?–399?], and the last poem was composed in A.D. 759.) A large number of the poems are folk ballads. They were written in Chinese characters, primarily for rendering Japanese syllables. This kind of writing system is called *Man'yo-gana*, or *Man'yo* style *kana* (Japanese syllabary), which was replaced by the fully developed *kana* syllabary during the Heian period.

The contents of the poems are classifiable as three kinds: (1) poems on miscellaneous topics including love of nature, observations of everyday life, historical sites, traveling, legends, and banquets; (2) *somon* (poems exchanged between two individuals) including love poems between man and woman, and poems expressing affection toward one's children, brothers, and sisters; (3) *banka* (eulogies) and elegies. *Banka* were originally chanted by those who followed the coffin to the gravesite, and many are moving expressions of grief over the loss of the beloved.

As to the form of the poems in *Man'yoshu*, there are *tanka* (short poems) and *choka* (long poems). Tanka are also referred to as *waka* (Japanese poems), because this form has become the mainstream of poetry in Japan. The over-whelming majority of the poems (about 4,200 in all) in *Man'yoshu* are tanka. In both tanka and choka, rhyme is avoided and the number of syllables in each line (verse) is the most important factor for the rhythm of the poem. A standard tanka has 31 syllables altogether, divided into two units. The first unit contains three lines with 5, 7, and 5 syllables, and the latter unit contains two lines with 7 syllables each. For example:

Yuusareba
Ogura no yama ni
naku shika wa
koyoi wa nakazu
ineni kerashimo

The stag of the Ogura mountain
    that cries when evening comes,
cries not tonight—
Is that he sleeps?[2]

Poem by the Jomei emperor

Man'yoshu contains some 260 *choka* (long poems). A standard choka con-tains a series of two-line units, each made up of a 5- followed by a 7-syllable line. The poet uses as many of these units as he or she wishes and concludes with a final 7-syllable line. A choka is often followed by one or more tanka as envoy(s) or refrain(s) that correspond with the contents of the preceding long poem. There is another form of poems called *sedoka*. Some sixty of the long poems in *Man'yoshu* are identified as sedoka, which is a variation of the long poem with three-line units composed of a 5- followed by a 7- and then another 7-syllable line, with as many units as the poet chooses.

The following is an example of a choka followed by a tanka:

"ON A DISTANT VIEW OF MOUNT FUJI"

Ametsuchi no
wakareshi toki yu
kamusabite
takaku toutoki
Suruga naru
Fuji no takane wo
Amanohara
furisakemireba
wataru hi no
kage mo kakuroi
teru tsuki no
hikari mo miezu
shirakumo mo
iyuki habakari
tokijikuzo
yuki wa furikeru
kataritsugi
iitsugi yukan
Fuji no takane wa

Tago no ura yu
uchiidete mireba
mashironi zo
Fuji no takane ni
yuki wa furikeru

Ever since heaven and earth were parted,
    It has towered lofty, noble, divine,
Mount Fuji in Suruga!

When we look up to the plains of heaven,
The light of the sky-traversing sun is shaded,
The gleam of the shining moon is not seen,
White clouds dare not cross it,
And for ever it snows.
We shall tell of it from mouth to mouth,
O the lofty mountain of Fuji!

　　[Envoy]
When going forth I look far from the shore of Tago,
How white and glittering is
The lofty Peak of Fuji,
Crowned with snows![3]

Poem by YAMABE no Akahito

Emperors' poems typically represent very positive views of their realm. A poem by the Jomei emperor (r. A.D. 629–641) viewing the stretch of the Yamato Plain from a hilltop is a song of praise and joy over the land he ruled:

Yamato ni wa/ murayama aredo/yoriyorou/ Ame-no-Kaguyama/
noboritachi/ kumini wo sureba/ kunibara wa/ keburi tabitatsu/
unabara wa/ kamame tachitatsu/
umashi kunizo/ Akitsushima/ Yamato no kuniwa

Countless are the mountains in Yamato,
　But perfect is the heavenly hill of Kagu;
When I climb it and survey my realm,
Over the wide plain the smoke-wreaths rise and rise,
Over the wide lake the gulls are on the wing;
A beautiful land it is, the Land of Yamato![4]

Poem by the Jomei emperor

Among the Man'yo poets whose names are known, there were many court nobles and their consorts. Princess Nukata was the consort of the Tenji emperor (r. 668–671) and also a lover of the future Temmu emperor (r. 672–686). She wrote passionate poems reflecting her turbulent love life. KAKINOMOTO no Hitomaro was a courtier who contributed many long poems, some in praise of the beauty and prosperity of the realm of the emperor. Yamabe no Akahito served the Shomu emperor (r. 724–749) as a lower-ranking courtier and excelled in writing nature poems. His poem of Mount Fuji, cited above, is the best known.

YAMANOUE no Okura (660?–733?) was a lower-ranking aristocrat who was sent on a mission to China and thereafter was appointed as an official in Kyushu. He contributed long poems describing everyday life, the misery of poverty and old age, and passionate love toward his children and wife. The following is a translation of his famous poem entitled "Thinking of Children":

> When I eat melon,
>   I remember my children;
> When I eat chestnuts,
> Even more do I recall them.
> Whence did they come to me?
> Before my eyes they will linger,
> And I cannot sleep in peace.[5]

Poem by Yamanoue no Okura

OTOMO no Tabito (665?–731), who headed the powerful Otomo clan, had a high rank as a nobleman, and served as a minister at the imperial court, and his half-sister, OTOMO no Sakanoue no Iratsume, were among the leading poets of their time. OTOMO no Yakamochi (718?–785), a son of Otomo no Tabito, was the most prolific poet in the *Man'yoshu*. He contributed at least 370 poems to the collection. He is presumed to be the final compiler of the *Man'yoshu*, which had been gathered by a number of people over a long stretch of time. His famous poem, "In Praise of Sake" reveals the Japanese attitude toward *sake* drinking, which seems not have changed much until very recently. The poem also shows the influence of the Buddhist outlook shared by many other contemporary poets.

> Instead of wasting thoughts on unavailing thing,
>   It would seem wiser
> To drink a cup of raw sake.

> Far better, it seems, than uttering pompous words
> And looking wise,
> To drink sake and weep drunken tears.

Grotesque! When I look upon a man
Who drinks no sake, looking wise,
How like an ape he is!

Among the countless ways of pleasure
What refreshes most
Is weeping drunken tears!

If I could but be happy in this life,
What should I care if in the next
I become a bird or a worm!

All living things die in the end:
So long as I live here
I want the cup of pleasure.

Silence with the airs of wisdom
Is far worse
Than weeping drunken tears![6]

Poem by Otomo no Yakamochi

Poems by outstanding Man'yo poets are familiar to the general public in Japan. The poems cited above are some of the best known. Little is known about the lives of most of the poets, but many of them were lower-rank aristocrats or courtiers who practiced poetry as a kind of profession. Also there were quite a few women poets. The most outstanding were Princess Nukata and Lady Otomo Sakanoue.

Free-spirited expression of emotion, such as love between man and woman, sometimes even between man and married woman, unrestrained grievance over the death of the beloved, and joys and sorrows in daily life— these are characteristic of poems in *Man'yoshu*. In later poems, expressions tended to be stylized. Also, in later times the *Man'yoshu* tradition of participation by various folks in poetry, including peasants and soldiers, was discontinued.

During the Heian period (A.D. 794–1185), *kana* (Japanese syllabary, or a set of phonetic symbols) were invented and spread among aristocratic women, who became important contributors to Heian literature. Poetry played an important role in the daily life of aristocrats and monks (i.e., retired aristocrats who took Buddhist vows), being a means of communication between individuals—especially between lovers. Love affairs began with sending a poem written in fine brush writing. During the courtship, the man sent a poem after each visit to his lover. The woman sent her reply in a poem. In the novel *The Tale of Genji*, there are about eight hundred poems.

Poems of the Heian aristocrats (and their descendants) as a whole had a tone of melancholy. Their favorite themes were fading cherry blossoms and falling autumn leaves. Both symbolized the impermanence of life. Awareness of the intrinsic sadness of things, which was expressed in the term *mono-no-aware* (sadness of things) ran throughout Heian literature and art. Among the outstanding poets in this tradition were ARIWARA no Narihira, an early Heian aristocrat; ONO no Komachi and IZUMI Shikibu, court ladies; and Priest Saigyo, who had served at the imperial court as a gentleman-in-waiting before he took Buddhist vows and, as a free-minded poet, traveled throughout the country.

The following are examples of famous poems from the Heian period.

    Hanano iro wa
Utsurinikeri na
    Itazura ni
Waga mi yo ni furu
Nagame seshi ma ni

The color of the [cherry] blossoms,
Faded away,
While I was watching the long rain,
Growing old in this world.[7]

Poem by ONO no Komachi

    Hisakata no
Hikari nodokeki
    Haru no hi ni
Shizugokoro naku
Hana no chiruran

The gentle light of spring
Fills the sky all over.
On such a tranquil day,
Why do the cherry blossoms
Shed their petals restlessly[8]?

Poem by KI no Tomonori

Kokoro naki
Mi ni mo aware wa
   Shirarekeri
Shigi tatsu sawa no
Aki no yugure

Even a priest [as I am]
who forsook passions of this world
cannot but be touched by the melancholy beauty
Of the marsh in the autumn dusk
Where a longbill flies off.[9]

Poem by Priest Saigyo

During the Heian period an anthology of poems, *Kokinshu* (or *Kokin wakashu,* Collection of Ancient and Modern Poetry, A.D. 905), was compiled under imperial order. The collection contained 1,100 poems, most of which are *tanka.* Long poems became increasingly rare until a new form of poetry was created in the nineteenth century. The chief compiler of *Kokinshu,* KI no Tsurayuki, himself was a renowned poet, and his preface to the collection is recognized as the first major piece of literary criticism written in Japanese. Another imperially commissioned anthology, *Shin kokinshu* (New Collection of Ancient and Modern Poetry, A.D. 1205), is counted as one of the three greatest anthologies of Japanese poems (together with *Man'yoshu* and *Kokinshu*). After these models, nineteen more anthologies of poems were compiled under imperial order, and the last anthology was completed in 1439. Also, many private anthologies were compiled and circulated among educated circles.

Aesthetic ideals of medieval Japan (i.e., from around the twelfth through sixteenth century) were expressed in such terms as *aware* (sorrow; gentle melancholy), *wabi* (forlornness), *sabi* (restrained beauty; literally, rust), *yugen* (subtle profundity), and *miyabi* (courtly elegance). These concepts were explained in treatises on *noh* drama by Zeami (1363–1443?) of Kanze troupe and his son-in-law, Zenchiku (1405–1470?) of Komparu theater.

Kanshi (Chinese Poems)

During the Nara period and the early Heian period when the Japanese eagerly learned from the sophisticated culture of Tang Dynasty China (618–907), Chinese classics and literature became the mainstay of aristocratic men's cultivation. To be an educated man, one had to be able to read and write in classic Chinese. Although famous poems were written in *kana* during the Heian period and thereafter, male members of the aristocracy wrote Chinese poems, or *kanshi* in Japanese. SUGAWARA no Michizane (845–903), who once served as a high-ranking minister, is well known for his skill in writing Chinese poems.

Kaifuso (Poems in Reminiscence, 751) is the oldest surviving collection of *kanshi*. The tradition of writing Chinese poems following Chinese literary conventions continued throughout Japanese history and regained popularity during the Meiji era as an art of educated men.

Renga (Linked Verses)

Renga (linked verses) is a group art developed during the late thirteenth and fourteenth centuries. It became a popular pastime not only for aristocratic poets but also for common folk who began to participate in literary activities. For artistic quality, best known are the linked verses led by Sogi (A.D. 1421–1502), a *renga* master who traveled all over the country to promote this art among aristocrats and warriors.

Initially the practice involved composing a *tanka* (short poem) by two people. That is, the first person wrote the opening three lines in 5–7–5 syllables, and the other wrote the final two lines in 7–7 syllables. Later the practice developed into a long chain of verses when a third person added another unit of 5–7–5 syllables, which was to be completed by the first person with a unit of 7–7 syllable lines. In this way a group of three or more (usually up to about ten people) kept linking new verses in turn before capping the poem with two ending lines. The participants enjoyed contributing witty responses to each other's verses while aiming at creating a scroll-like effect by developing unifying themes.[10]

Complex rules evolved concerning verses that could be linked. For example, it was required that the opening three lines contain some word indicating one of the four seasons. Participants in a *renga* circle strove to outdo each other with their technical skill. Thus the entire process was prone to become a literary game.

Haiku (Haikai or Hokku)

Haiku is the shortest form of poetry, consisting of three lines with 5, 7, and 5 syllables each. It is a light-hearted poetry that started as the opening verse of *renga* (see above). It was also called *haikai* or *hokku* in its early history, but now it is known as *haiku*. This poetic form became very popular among townsmen during the Tokugawa period. As Donald Keene has pointed out, Japanese valued "the power of suggestion" of brief poems that were free of descriptive details.[11] The following example is one of the most famous haiku by MATSUO Basho:

Furuike ya
Kawazu tobikomu
Mizu no oto

(An old pond,
A frog jumps in;
The sound of the water.)[12]

Haiku by MATSUO Basho

Matsuo Basho (1644–1694) is regarded as the greatest master of haiku. In his conversations with his disciples, Basho pointed out that haiku must be both eternal and momentary. Haiku is an art of brevity, capturing the eternity in a moment of reality of life. It is almost like an enlightenment in Zen meditation that comes as a sudden flash of intuition. The reality expressed in a haiku is the brevity of life within the everlasting cycle of nature, and therefore it must contain a word that indicates the season. "Frog" in the above example suggests late spring. In contrast to *tanka*, in which elegant expressions are favored to convey delicate sensibility, preferred expressions in haiku are realistic and concrete representations of daily life. They were often humorous. Instead of flower or leaf, haiku could be focused on cicada, frog, fly, monkey or anything that represents a creature in the familiar environment of everyday life.[13]

Basho was born in a samurai family but took Buddhist vows to renounce his status and traveled extensively in a monk's robe. His travel diary, *Oku no hosomichi* (The Narrow Road of Oku, 1694) is a collection of his haiku written at scenic places where he stopped to make literary sketches. After Basho, YOSA Buson (1716–1783), who was also a landscape painter, and KOBAYASHI Issa (1763–1827), a commoner who was good at depicting commoners' lives, are considered great haiku poets of the Tokugawa period. Haiku was very popular among townsmen, whereas the tradition of *waka* was regarded as a high-brow activity maintained by imperial court nobles, monks, educated elite among military rulers, and their wives.

Diaries

The diary was an important genre of *kana* literature that developed during the Heian period (A.D. 794–1185). *Tosa nikki* (Tosa Diary, 935) by KI no Tsurayuki is an outstanding early example. This is a travel diary he kept while traveling from the province of Tosa, where he served as governor, back to his home in Kyoto. It was written in *kana* against the custom of the day when men were supposed to write prose, including diary entries, in Chinese. To compromise with that convention, the author invented a fictitious female character as the narrator of the diary. All other surviving diaries from the Heian and Kamakura periods were written by women. *Sarashina nikki* (Sarashina Diary, 1059–1060) was written by the daughter of Sugawara no Takasue who traveled from Sarashina in Shinano province to Kyoto and became a lady-in-waiting at the imperial court. *Kagero nikki* (Gossamer Diary, 990), by the estranged wife of a prime minister, is filled with her bitterness and resentment. *Murasaki Shikibu nikki* (Diary of Murasaki Shikibu, ca. 1010), by the author of *The Tale of Genji*, depicts daily life in the empress's court. *Izumi Shikibu nikki* (Diary of Izumi Shikibu, 1007) was supposedly written by a romantic poetess, IZUMI Shikibu, but possibly by some unknown author who pretended to be Izumi Shikibu. The diary genre was also used as a form of fiction. During the Kamakura period, *Izayoi nikki* (Diary of the Waning Woman, 1280) was written by Abutsuni, a court lady turned nun.

The method of applying the form of diary for writing fiction was used by modern writers. TANIZAKI Jun'ichiro's novel about an old man's sex fantasy, *Kagi* (The Key, 1956), is an outstanding example.

Essays

Essay was another genre developed as a *kana* literature during the Heian period. The most prominent collection from this period is *Makura no soshi* (Pillow Book, ca. 1002) by SEI Shonagon, who is regarded as one of the two greatest writers of the Heian period (together with Murasaki Shikibu, author of *The Tale of Genji*). Both women writers lived as court ladies in service of the empress at the time when aristocratic culture was at its peak. In her essays in *Makura no soshi*, Sei Shonagon commented on various things and people she observed around the empress's court and described the events of every season of the year. She was a keen observer of people's behavior and expressed her critical viewpoints with a humorous touch. Some essays are several pages long, and others are just a few sentences. The following are examples of her short essays:

"ON THE THIRD DAY OF THE THIRD MONTH"

On the third day of the Third Month I like to see the sun shining bright and calm in the spring sky. Now is the time when the peach trees come into bloom, and what a sight it is! The willows too are most charming at this season, with the buds still enclosed like silkworms in their cocoons. After the leaves have spread out, I find them unattractive; in fact all trees lose their charm once the blossoms have begun to scatter.

It is a great pleasure to break off a long, beautifully flowering branch from a cherry tree and to arrange it in a large vase. What a delightful task to perform when a visitor is seated nearby conversing! It may be an ordinary guest, or possibly one of Their Highnessess, the Empress's elder brothers; but in any case the visitor will wear a cherry-colored Court cloak, from the bottom of which his under-robe emerges. I am even happier if a butterfly or a small bird flutters prettily near the flowers and I can see its face.[14]

"DIFFERENT WAYS OF SPEAKING"

A priest's language.

The speech of men and women.

The common people always tend to add extra syllables to their
   words.[15]

After the Heian period, the political and cultural center of Japan shifted away from the imperial court in Kyoto. For four centuries following the end of the Heian period, until the establishment of the Tokugawa regime in Edo (present-day Tokyo) in 1600, political and cultural authority was fragmented. Civil wars and uneasy peace became the norm. During this period the influence of Buddhist philosophy became prevalent. Military lords and Buddhist monasteries provided sanctuary to men of letters. Many accomplished writers were old aristocrats who renounced this world by taking Buddhist vows.

KAMO no Chomei, a former courtier who took Buddhist vows, wrote *Hojoki* (Essays of the Ten-Foot-Square Hut, 1212), in which he reflected on the change from aristocratic society to warrior-dominated world.

Tsurezuregusa (Essays in Idleness, 1330–1331), by YOSHIDA Kenko, is another famous collection written by a Buddhist recluse. Before he had his head shaved to become a Buddhist priest, he was a gentleman-in-waiting at the court of a cloistered emperor and was a renowned poet. In his resignation from this world, he contemplated the ideal way to live. The following is one of his well-known essays:

If man were never to fade away like the dews of Adashino (a graveyard), never to vanish like the smoke over Toribeyama (where the bodies were cremated) but lingered on forever in the world, how things would lose their power to move us! The most precious thing in life is its uncertainty. Consider living creatures—none lives so long as man. The May fly waits not for the evening, the summer cicada knows neither spring nor autumn. What a wonderfully unhurried feeling it is to live even a single year in perfect serenity! If that is not enough for you, you might live a thousand years and still feel it was but a single night's dream. We cannot live for ever in this world; why should we wait for ugliness to overtake us? The longer man lives, the more shame he endures. To die, at the latest, before one reaches forty, is the least unattractive. Once a man passes that age, he desires (with no sense of shame over his appearance) to mingle in the company of others. In his sunset years he dotes on his grandchildren, and prays for long life so that he may see them prosper. His preoccupation with worldly desires grows ever deeper, and gradually he loses all sensitivity to the beauty of things, a lamentable state of affairs.[16]

Fiction

Monogatari (Tales)

The *Genji monogatari* (The Tale of Genji, ca. 1002–1019) is the greatest among many *monogatari* written during the Heian period. It is regarded not only as the masterpiece of classical Japanese fiction but also as the earliest novel of world literature. It is a fictional story of the romantic life of Prince Genji written in *kana* in fifty-four books (chapters). The author, MURA-SAKI Shikibu, was a lady-in-waiting at an empress's court at the time of the peak of the Fujiwara family, from which the empress came. The first page begins with the story of Prince Genji's mother, a lady-in-waiting at the court of an emperor whose time or reign period is not identified. Prince Genji is a personification of the ideal nobleman in terms of personal beauty, elegance, talent in music and poetry, and sensibility. Although the emperor favored this prince the most, he was not considered an heir apparent because of the low rank of his mother and the lack of powerful grandparents on his mother's side (which was essential to secure the position as heir apparent). In every chapter, each of his love affairs is narrated with sympathetic description of the appearance and personality of the women. The last ten chapters describe the tragic life of his son. *The Tale of Genji* was read widely, not only by contemporaries but by successive generations up to modern times. Regarded as a model of romantic fiction, it influenced many writers. There are several versions of translations of this story in modern Japanese, as well as English translations by Arthur Waley (1925) and Edward Seidensticker (1976).

Various other kinds of tales were also written during the Heian period. *Taketori monogatari* (Tale of a Bamboo Cutter), written in the ninth century, is a fantasy story of a fairy princess who was found in a bamboo stalk by a child-less bamboo cutter, was raised by the bamboo cutter and his wife to be a beauty, and was sought after by many noblemen, but she rejected them all. In the end she returned to her palace on the moon, leaving behind the elderly couple.

During the Kamakura period, several accounts of great historical events were written. Among them, *Heike monogatari* (Tale of the House of Taira, or Heike; early thirteenth century) is outstanding. It was originally chanted by blind storytellers with accompaniment of *biwa* (four-string lute). It narrates the events from 1132 to 1213 focusing on the fall of the warrior house of Taira (Heike) from the height of power and glory in their battle with the house of Minamoto (Genji), who founded the military government in Kamakura in 1192. The recurrent theme of the story is the impermanence of glory.

Many other historical narratives written during the Kamakura period lament the destruction of civilized life and the misery of the chaotic age.

Ghost Stories and Other Short Stories

From the late Heian period through the Muromachi period, various collections of short stories were compiled. These may have been orally narrated at first. Ghost stories, miracle stories of Buddhist or Shinto deities, had didactic messages for the commoners. *Nihon ryoiki* (miraculous stories from the Japanese Buddhist tradition, written from the fifth to the ninth centuries) and *Uji shui shu* (a collection of tales from Uji, written in the early thirteenth century) are best-known examples. Hundreds of short stories written from the fourteenth to seventeenth centuries, and generally categorized as *otogi zoshi* (once-told tales) are known. They are tales of noblemen, warriors, priests, commoners, and animals; many are success stories from the chaotic age. Many fairy tales for children in Japan today are adapted from these stories. Everyone in Japan knows the stories of "Battle of Monkey and Crab," "The Boy Who Was Born of a Peach," "One-Inch-Tall Samurai Monk," and "Old Man Who Brought Blossoms on a Dead Cherry Tree." Children in Japan hear these stories read by their parents or, nowadays, see them on television as animated cartoons. The heroes and heroines are just as famous as Snow White or Cinderella.

Novels of Townsmen in the Tokugawa Era

After Tokugawa Ieyasu put all other feudal lords under his control in 1600, there were no more civil wars to produce military heroes for storytellers to praise. Warriors under the Tokugawa regime became civil bureaucrats. Their education was essentially in Chinese classics, and they aspired to write poems in classical Chinese, or at least *waka* in classical Japanese. They were not interested in popular literature for entertainment. The worlds of samurai and of commoners were quite separate.

The new heroes and heroines of fiction in the Tokugawa period were merchants, artisans, their family members and servants, and entertainers, who were collectively called "town's men." They were placed at the bottom of the social hierarchy, in which the samurai occupied the top position and the farmers, the producers of primary goods, occupied the second. Despite their lowly social station, the townsmen prospered—especially after the economic boom around the turn of the eighteenth century. This is identified as the Genroku boom, after the reign title of Genroku, 1688–1704.

It was during the Genroku era that the *haiku* master Matsuo Basho lived. His followers were primarily townsmen, among whom the *renga*, or linked verse poetry, was very popular. The first important novelist of the Tokugawa era, IHARA Saikaku (1642–1693), also lived in the Genroku era. Saikaku was born in a wealthy merchant house in Osaka and was an expert in *renga*, which he took up as a hobby. Later he was devoted to writing novels, leaving the family business in the hands of his managers. He wrote many novels, but the best were stories of commoners who lived in cities. He was the first important novelist to write about the lives of townsmen. Moreover, his novels were for the entertainment of the townsmen, whose interests were money and sex. *Koshoku ichidai otoko* (The Man Who Spent His Life at Love Making) is a story of the sexual experiences of Yonosuke, a character Saikaku created that later became a stereotype. Between the ages of 7 and 60, Yonosuke is said to have dallied with 3,742 women and frolicked with 725 boys. The organization of this novel is modeled after the chapters of *The Tale of Genji*, but he was not interested in describing the psychology of romantic love; he described only circumstances and actions. *Koshoku gonin onna* (Five Women Who Loved Love) is a series of tragic love stories about townswomen that were based on real events. Saikaku also wrote *Nanshoku okagami* (The

Great Mirror of Love between Men). His novels had great commercial success. *Nippon eitaigura* (The Japanese Family Storehouse) and *Seken munazan'yo* (Reckonings That Carry Men through the World) are biographical stories of merchants focusing on their business career. A typical hero of Saikaku's comedy or tragedy is a man who builds a fortune by hard work and sharp wit, and later spends all of it at the "pleasure quarters."

During the Tokugawa period, most townsmen's philosophy of life was hedonistic. For them, life was *ukiyo* (floating world), which was best spent in lighthearted pleasures. For the Heian period aristocrats, *ukiyo* meant "sorrowful world," and their ideal was to cultivate sensitivity to touch the beauty in nature. For Edo townsmen, the ideal of a cultivated man was expressed in the word *iki*, which could be translated as "smart" or "cool" in American slang. A man of *iki* cares about his appearance without being noticed for his efforts. He spends his money on clothes of the latest fashion and other trendy things, and indeed he has good taste. He does not show any concern over money, even if he is very poor. The opposite of *iki* is *yabo* (rusticated, dumb, too serious, stingy).

After Saikaku, many more stories about townsmen were written for the entertainment of townsmen. JUPPENSHA Ikku's story of travel on the Tokaido highway is well known. The greatest achievement in Tokugawa literature was in drama. CHIKAMATSU Monzaemon wrote scenarios for both *kabuki* and puppet theater.

MODERN LITERATURE

Poetry

Shi (Kindaishi)

Modern poetry, characterized by free verse without restrictions on the number of syllables or lines, modern vocabulary, and even colloquial language, was developed in Japan during the nineteenth century under the influence of such European literary trends as Romanticism and Symbolism. The earliest publication of modern poetry, *Shintaishi sho* (Collection of Selected Modern Poems, 1882), contained translations of English and German poems by scholars at Tokyo Imperial University. UEDA Bin's (1874–1916) translation of French poems gained fame for its elegant style. Early modern poetry is referred to as *shintaishi, juyushi,* or *kindaishi* to distinguish it from traditional Japanese poetry (*waka,* or *uta*) or Chinese poetry (*kanshi*). Today it is referred to as *shi.*

To nurture the development of modern poetry, Shinshisha (New Poetry

Society, founded by YOSANO Tekkan in 1899) was very important. It provided a forum not only for modern *tanka* but also for the new-style poetry. KITAHARA Hakushu (1885–1943), KAMBARA Ariake (1876–1952), SU-SUKIDA Kyukin (1877–1945), TAKAMURA Kotaro (1883–1956), and HAGIWARA Sakutaro (1886–1942) were among the popular poets of modern style who started out as *tanka* poets.

Waka in Modern Language

During the Meiji era, the creation of a new-style poetry after the model of modern European poems was the most noteworthy development. However, traditional *waka* also regained popularity. Waka poets who promoted the movement to reform waka organized literary associations and published literary magazines for their poems. They expressed their new ideas in the traditional format with 31 syllables. OCHIAI Naobumi (1861–1903), a poet and scholar, was one of the earliest to start this movement. Yosano Tekkan (1873–1935) formed Shinshisha (New Poetry Society) and published its journal, *Myojo* (Bright Star), in 1899. Joined by Yosano Akiko (1878–1952) who was married to Tekkan, and other young poets, this group gained great popularity and influence in popularizing the new ideas in Japanese-style poetry. Their orientation was characterized as Romantic. Many prominent poets started their literary careers with this group.

Another group of poets who preferred the straightforward style of the *Man'yoshu* and Realism formed a group, Araragi, in 1908, under the leadership of ITO Sachio (1864–1913), a novelist and poet, and SAITO Mokichi (1882–1953), who was not only a poet but also a medical doctor. They were followers of MASAOKA Shiki (1867–1902), an earlier advocate of reform in *tanka* and *haiku*.

Aside from these very influential groups, numerous associations of poets were organized, subdivided, disbanded, and reorganized. Literary magazines and collections of poems were published, and many poems were frequently cited in everyday life by ordinary people. KITAHARA Hakushu (1885–1943), ISHIKAWA Takuboku (1886–1912), and TSUCHIYA Bummei (1890–1990) were very well known to the general public.

The tradition of *tanka* (short poem) remained strong throughout the modern era. In the 1990s, a collection of tanka by a young woman poet, TA-WARA Machi (1962–   ), appeared on the list of best-sellers. Her poems reflect very familiar scenes in daily life and honest feelings of urban middle-class people in modern cities. An example below comes from the poems written on a trip to Paris with her intimate companion. Here she expresses new taste in the traditional form of tanka:

Just to buy a baguette and milk
In this simplicity
starts our morning,
You and I, together alone.[17]

Translation of a *tanka* by Tawara Machi

Fiction

To create the genre of modern fiction in late nineteenth-century Japan, it was necessary to establish not only a new literary style but also a new written language that could express modern realities and ethical values. This task was carried out by scholars trained in modern European languages. TSUBOU-CHI Shoyo (1859–1935), who graduated from Tokyo Imperial University and later became a professor at Waseda University, published a very important treatise on the modern novel in 1885. He founded an influential literary magazine, *Waseda Bungaku* (Waseda Literature, 1891–1898). In his later years he completed a translation of the collected works of William Shakespeare.

FUTABATEI Shimei (1864–1909), who was trained in Russian language and literature, wrote a novel entitled *Ukigumo* (Drifting Clouds, 1887–1889), which has been regarded as the first successful modern novel in Japan. Another pioneer of modern fiction, OZAKI Koyo (1867–1903), wrote *Konjiki yasha* (The Misers, 1898–1903) and other popular novels. He was the leader of the influential literary coterie Kenyusha (Friends of Inkstone). KODA Rohan (1867–1947), who wrote *Goju no to* (Five-Story Pagoda, 1891), also pioneered modern fiction.

Because successful authors of modern fiction enjoyed prestige and commanded moral leadership in early twentieth-century Japan, the entire generation of talented young men (and some women) aspired to become writers. The following are the most prominent.

HIGUCHI Ichiyo (1872–1896) was a short-lived woman writer of humble origin who brilliantly depicted the life and ethos of unprivileged residents of Tokyo. Her *Takekurabe* (1895–1896, translated as "Growing Up") is about adolescents who worked as servants in the Yoshiwara district of Tokyo.

SHIMAZAKI Toson (1871–1943) started as a poet and turned out to be an accomplished fiction writer. His first novel, *Hakai* (1906, translated as *The Broken Commandment*), was about a *burakumin* (traditional outcast whose offspring still suffer from discrimination). It is regarded as a landmark in the history of modern Japanese Realism. His *Ie* (1910–1911, translated as *The Family*) and *Shinsei* (New Life, 1918–1919) also depicted bleak realities of Japanese society in transition. His final work, *Yoakemae* (1929–1935, translated as *Before the Dawn*), is a historical novel about the rapid changes in Japanese society during the Meiji period.

MORI Ogai (1862–1922) was a medical doctor trained at Tokyo Imperial University, head of the army medical corps, a German scholar, translator, critic, historian, and novelist. His early novel, *Maihime* (1890, translated as *The Dancing Girl*), is about the short-lived love affair of a Japanese youth studying in Berlin with a German dancing girl. *Gan* (1911–1913, translated as *The Wild Geese*) is about a usurer's mistress who falls in love with a student at an elite university. In his later years, Ogai wrote historical novels.

NATSUME Soseki (1867–1916), whose portrait is printed on 1000-yen bills, was perhaps the most famous novelist in modern Japan. A graduate of Tokyo Imperial University, he was sent to England to study and, upon his return, taught at the university for a brief period. From his first novel, *Wagahai wa neko de aru* (1905–1906, translated as *I Am a Cat*), to his last, *Meian* (1916; translated as *Light and Darkness*), the heroes of his novels are almost always university-educated men who are vulnerable to loneliness and uncertainty in the modern age. *Kusamakura* (1905, translated as *The Three-Cornered World*), *Sanshiro* (1908, translated as *Sanshiro), Sorekara* (And Then, 1909), *Kokoro* (The Heart, 1914; title of a translation is *Kokoro), Mon* (The Gate, 1910; translation, *Mon*), and *Kojin* (1912–1913, translated as *The Wayfarer*) are the most popular of his novels.

Among prominent writers who were active from the 1920s through the 1950s, SHIGA Naoya (1883–1971) excelled in short stories. *An'yakoro* (1921–1937, translated as *A Dark Night Passing*) is his only long novel.

NAGAI Kafu (1879–1959), a prodigal son of a former samurai who became a successful bureaucrat, held on to his individualistic aestheticism against the growing pressure of the Socialist writers' movement and militarism. In *Bokuto kidan* (1937, translated as *A Strange Tale from East of the River*) and other short stories, he depicted the fading beauty of the old brothel area on the bank of the Sumida River in Tokyo where he spent much of his time. He also lived in New York and Paris for five years and wrote stories based on his real and imagined experiences in these cities.

TANIZAKI Jun'ichiro (1886–1965) was another artist of antiquarian taste but lacked financial resources. He had to withdraw from Tokyo Imperial University because he was unable to pay the tuition. He articulated an aestheticism that was nurtured in the old downtown district of Tokyo where he was born, and later in Osaka where he settled with his third wife. He depicted men who were enslaved by feminine beauty in *Chijin no ai* (A Fool's Love, 1924–1925) and *Tade kuu mushi* (1928–1929, translated as *Some Prefer*

Nettles, 1955). His *Sasameyuki* (Fine Snow, 1943–1948, translated as *The Makioka Sisters*) describes love and marriage in a middle-class family. *Kagi* (1956, translated as *The Key*) and *Futen rojin nikki* (1961–1962, translated as *Diary of a Mad Man*) are about an old man with a sexual obsession.

AKUTATAWA Ryunosuke (1892–1927) articulated cultural confusion and identity problems of the Taisho period (1912–1926) in his short stories and captured the imagination of middle-class intellectuals long after his suicide at age 35. Among his stories, "Rashomon" (1915; translation, *Rashomon*, 1952) and "Jigokuhen" (1918, translated as *The Hell Screen*) became world famous because of KUROSAWA Akira's movies based on these stories.

DAZAI Osamu (1909–1948), the son of a large landowner in northeastern Japan, was involved in an illegal Marxist political movement while he was studying French literature at Tokyo Imperial University, and he left the movement by giving himself up to the police. His *Shayo* (Setting Sun, 1947) reflected the confusion of moral values in a society defeated in war. It also expressed his own deep sense of failure, as well as his indulgence in narcissism and decadent sensuality. His last work, *Ningen shikkaku* (Unworthy to Be Human, 1948), reflected his guilt at betraying the expectations of his family and then of his comrades. Shortly after he wrote it, Dazai ended his life in suicide. The date of his death is still commemorated by young men and women of literary inclinations.

KAWABATA Yasunari (1899–1972) was awarded the Nobel Prize for Literature in 1968. He was the second Asian laureate after Rabindranath Tagore of India. His stories center on a man who espouses lyrical aestheticism and has a nihilistic outlook. *Yukiguni* (1935–1941, translated as *Snow Country)*, *Sembazuru* (1949–1951, translated as *A Thousand Cranes,*) and *Yama no oto* (1949–1954, translated as *Sound of the Mountain*) are his major works.

Of the writers who belong to the postwar generation, the following are among the most widely recognized. Reflecting the confidence the Japanese gained by their economic success, these writers reasserted traditional values and at the same time strove to answer universal questions regarding the human condition.

MISHIMA Yukio (1925–1970) authored *Kinkakuji* (1956, translated as *The Temple of the Golden Pavilion*) to describe the mind of a man who set the Golden Pavilion, a national treasure, on fire because of his obsession with its beauty. Mishima praised Japanese swordsmanship and martial spirit. To convey his message to the nation, he gave a passionate speech at the headquarters of the Self Defense Forces and then, upon withdrawing to a back room, committed suicide by *seppuku* (also known as *harakiri* in colloquial language) with a samurai sword.

ABE Kobo (1924–1993) wrote *Suna no onna* (1962), translated as *The Woman of the Dunes*, which is about the helplessness of the individual overwhelmed by the organization.

OE Kenzaburo (1935–), recipient of the 1994 Nobel Prize for Literature, deserves special attention here. He speaks for the postwar generation who—as his translators, Paul St. John Mackintosh and Maki Sugiyama, have characterized—felt deep anger against their elders for meekly allowing the militarist adventure and the brutal treatment of innocent people by the military men. Oe's generation grew up amid the height of tension in the early years of the Cold War. This generation was troubled with the question of Japan's political identity between the two camps in the Cold War as well as its cultural identity between the East and the West.

Oe was born in 1935 in a village in an isolated area of Shikoku. His family was well-to-do and well established in the village, thanks to his father's official monopoly of the bark-stripping business. In 1954 he entered the University of Tokyo and studied French literature. He wrote stories for student magazines using the methods of French literature he was studying. In 1958 his story *Shiiku (Prize Stock)* won the Akutagawa Prize, Japan's most prestigious literary award for new writers. Oe was only 23 years old. In the same year, his *Memushiri kouchi* (translated as *Nip the Buds, Shoot the Kids*) was published. Oe left the University of Tokyo in 1959 with a graduation thesis on Jean-Paul Sartre. In 1960 he married Yukari, the sister of ITAMI Juzo (the film director of *Tampopo*), a friend from his school days in Shikoku, and settled down as a fulltime writer. His two serial stories of 1961 were based on the assassination in 1960 of the Socialist Party leader by a 17-year-old right-winger. This was the era of mass left-wing demonstrations against the renegotiation of Japan's security treaty with the United States. The demonstrations that filled the streets of Tokyo were fueled by strong sentiment against Japan's likely involvement in another war, this time with nuclear bombs.

Soon thereafter, Oe was struck by a tragic event. His first son was born in 1963 with a cerebral hernia. He named the boy Hikari (Light), as if to break through the darkness surrounding him and his family. His novel *Aru kojinteki na taiken* (1964, translated as *A Personal Matter*) is a record of his agonized struggle. *Hiroshima noto* (1964, translated as *Hiroshima Notes*) is a record of his interviews with and impressions of survivors of the atomic bomb in Hiroshima. *Man'en gannen no futtoboru* (1967, translated as *The Silent Cry*) opens with the birth of a deformed child and the death of a man who hangs himself, and it closes with the narrator's redemption. Oe also wrote *Dojidai gemu* (1979, translated as *Contemporary Games*) and *M/T to mor ino fushigi no monogatari* (1986, translated as *M/T and the Marvels of the Forest*), *Chiryoto* (1990, translated as *The Treatment Tower*), and many other novels. He readily gained international recognition.

In his Nobel lecture entitled "Japan, the Ambiguous, and Myself," Oe highlighted Japan's plight, riven by an "ambiguity so powerful and penetrating that it splits both the state and its people." In the words of the translators of Oe's novels, Paul St. John Mackintosh and Maki Sugiyama, "the ambiguous condition of his country, 'oriented toward learning from and imitating the West' since the onset of its modernization, yet an East Asian nation which 'has firmly maintained its traditional culture,' is for Oe a 'kind of chronic disease that has been prevalent throughout the modern age.' "[18] His most recent work is a trilogy, *Moeagaru midori no ki* (1993–1995, translated as *The Blazing Green Tree*).

Popular Fiction

Aside from "pure literature," which constitutes highly artistic and almost philosophical works, "popular literature" has become more respectable, and many superior works have been published in this new category. Certain works of popular fiction serialized in daily newspapers have become classics and made into movies or television dramas. Some deal with serious issues in contemporary society. Others are based on biographies of well-known historical figures. Among the authors who gained great popularity during the 1950s through the 1990s are ISHIZAKA Yojiro, OSARAGI Jiro, SHISHI Bunroku, ISHIKAWA Tatsuzo, ARIYOSHI Sawako, SONO Ayako, SETOUCHI Harumi (Jakusho), ENDO Shusaku, YAMAMOTO Shugoro, YAMAOKA Sohachi, SHIBA Ryotaro, TAKEDA Taijun, CHIN Shunshin, INOUE Yasushi, FUKAZAWA Shichiro, IKEDA Masuo, YOSHIMOTO Banana, MURAKAMI Ryu, and MURAKAMI Haruki. These writers have commanded nationwide attention in Japan, and many of their works have been translated into English.

Literary Associations and Literary Magazines

Important literary activities in Japan in the early twentieth century centered on associations that started out as coteries, or intimate small and often exclusive groups of writers with a common taste. Literary associations and their publications represented changing literary trends and at the same time shaped the literary power structure. In the early years of modern literature, the most influential associations and their publications were Shinshisha (New Poetry Society) and its journal, *Myojo* (Bright Star, 1900–1908), centered on *tanka*; the group headed by MASAOKA Shiki and later by TAKAHAMA Kyoshi (1874–1959) and its publication, *Hototogisu* (Nightingale, 1897–present), in the genre of *haiku*; and Kenyusha (Friends of Inkstone, 1885–1903) founded by OZAKI Koyo (1867–1903) and his associates who were fiction writers.

After World War II small literary circles continued to form, and they published numerous periodicals. As a result of the development of mass media after the war, however, literary associations ceased to play leading roles in literary activities. Unknown individuals now can emerge as best-selling writers and gain fame and status, such as ISHIHARA Shintaro in the 1950s. Today literary associations function as vocational organizations. The largest ones are Nihon Bungeika Kyokai (Japan Association of Writers, with over 1,000 members); the Japan P.E.N. Club; and Nihon Gendai Shijin Kai (Japan Modern Poets Society, with 400 members). In Japan today, numerous monthly periodicals publish short stories and novels in installments. Among them are *Bungei shunju, Bungakukai, Chuo koron, Shincho*, and *Gunzo*.

Literary Prizes

A common way for new writers, especially fiction writers, to get recognition is through winning literary prizes. Announcements of prizes are big events in the mass media, and recipients are given opportunities to publish their works for mass market. Among fifty some prizes, the most prestigious are the Akutagawa Prize and the Naoki Prize. Both were established in the 1930s by KIKUCHI Kan (1888–1948)—a writer, journalist, and later the president of publishing house, Bungei Shunju, Ltd.—for the purpose of recognizing promising writers. After his death, a prize in his name was created. The Dazai Osamu Prize, the Japan Art Academy Award, the Noma Literary Prize, the Mainichi Art Award, the Shincho Literary Prize, and the Tanizaki Jun'ichiro Prize are also prestigious prizes.

NOTES

1. In 1987, fully 36,346 new titles were published, of which 9,693 were classified as "literature and linguistics." Somucho Tokeikyoku, *1996 Sekai no Tokei* (1996 Statistics of the World) (Tokyo: Okurasho Insatsukyoku, 1996), p. 334.

2. Translation in *The Man'yoshu: The Nippon Gakujutsu Shinkokai Translation of One Thousand Poems* (New York: Columbia University Press, 1965), p. 3. All translations of poems in *The Man'yoshu* used with permission of the Japan Society for the Foundation of Science.

3. Translation in *Man'yoshu*, pp. 187–188.

4. Translation in *Man'yoshu*, pp. 3.

5. Translation in *Man'yoshu*, pp. 200–202.

6. Translation in *Man'yoshu*, pp. 117–118.

7. *Kokinshu*. The translation is mine. For a Japanese version, see Kaneko Mo-toomi, *Kokin waka shu hyoshaku (Annotated edition of Kokinshu)* (Tokyo: Meiji Shoin, 1927), p. 194.

8. *Kokinshu*. The translation is mine. For a Japanese version, see Kaneko Mo-toomi, *Kokin waka shu hyoshaku*, p. 170.

9. *Shin kokinshu*. Translation is mine. For a Japanese version, see Sasaki No-butsuna, eds., *Shin kokin waka shu*, Iwanami Bunko (Tokyo: Iwanami Shoten, 1929 [1944]), p. 69.

10. Donald Keene suggested the parallel between horizontal scroll (*emakimono*) and *renga* in his *Japanese Literature: An Introduction to Western Readers* (New York: Grove Press, 1955), pp. 37–38.

11. Keene, *Japanese Literature*, p. 28.

12. Matsuo Basho, "Haru no Hi (Spring Day)." The word-to-word translation is mine. For a Japanese edition, see Ito Sho-u, ed., *Basho shichibu shu (Seven collections of poems by Basho)*, Iwanami Bunko (Tokyo: Iwanami Shoten, 1927 [1936]), p. 36.

13. Keene, *Japanese Literature*, pp. 38–39.

14. Ivan Morris, trans., *Pillow Book of Sei Shonagon* (Baltimore, Md: Penguin Books, 1967), p. 24.

15. Ibid., p. 25.

16. Donald Keene, trans., *Essays in Idleness: Tsurezuregusa of Kenko* (New York: Columbia University Press, 1967), pp. 7–8.

17. From a series of poems under the title of "Wind on *Pont Neuf*" in Tawara Machi, *Chokoreito kakumei* (Chocolate Revolution) (Tokyo: Kawade Shobo Shinsha, 1997). The translation is mine.

18. Paul St. John Mackintosh and Maki Sugiyama, "Introduction," in Kenzaburo Oe, *Nip the Buds, Shoot the Kids* (London: Marion Boyards, 1995).

4

Art

PERFORMING ARTS: TRADITIONAL THEATER AND MUSIC

The major forms of traditional theatrical art that are still performed in Japan today are *bugaku, noh*, puppet theater known as *ningyo joruri* or *bunraku*, and *kabuki*. They are supported by a small number of well-educated and dedicated patrons, just as Italian opera is in the United States today. The repertoire of traditional performing art theaters in Japan today mostly consists of classic masterpieces. However, some attempts to create new pieces are being made by dramatists and performers.

Bugaku

Bugaku (literally, "dance music") is a type of *gagaku* (court music ensemble made up of stringed instruments, bamboo pipe instruments, drums, and, sometimes, singing) that is performed with dance. Gagaku was brought to Japan from Korea and China during the seventh and eighth centuries. The costume of the musicians and dancers is patterned after that of the Tang Dynasty in China (618–907). The dancers sometimes wear masks showing either human or animal faces. The tradition of gagaku was kept at the imperial court. Today, the Imperial Household Agency is in charge of the training and maintenance of the gagaku troops, which perform only for ceremonies at the imperial court and certain shrines.

Noh theater. Courtesy of Kyodo News.

Noh

Among the theatrical art publicly performed at theaters today, *noh* is the oldest and the most aristocratic. A combination of singing, dancing, and instrumental music, it was perfected in the fourteenth and fifteenth centuries by Kan'ami (1333–1384), the founder of the Kanze troupe, and his son, Zeami (also pronounced Seami) (1363–1443), as an art to express *yugen* (subtle profundity). Noh was favored by the elite among the warriors who ruled medieval Japan. Eventually the present form of noh was established during the sixteenth and seventeenth centuries.

The stage of noh theater is six meters square and is made of polished Japanese cypress. Pillars at the four corners support the shrine-like roof over the stage. On the back wall are painted a stylized pine tree and some bamboos. From the rear of the stage to its left, as seen by the audience, about 10 meters (32 feet) long and 3 meters wide, is a passageway called *hashigakari* extending to the dressing room. A stretch of white pebbles placed around the stage and the passageway separates the performance space from the audience. On the pebbles below the *hashigakari* are three pine trees placed at certain intervals and used as markers when the actors progress toward or retreat from the stage. A rear stage extends 3 meters on the back, and a side stage extends 1.5 meters on the right.

The noh stage is very simple, with no scenery except the painting of the pine tree and bamboos on the back wall. At times props, or *tsukurimono*, are used. For example, a house is represented very simply by four bamboo pillars supporting a roof. A robe lying on the stage represents a sick person in bed. Stage props in noh are symbolic.

The sound of a flute signals the beginning of the performance. Then, three or four musicians (called *hayashi-kata*) dressed in formal black costume enter through the passageway and sit at the rear end of the main stage. The instruments are *taiko* (large drum), *ozutsumi* (large hand drum), *kozutsumi* (small hand drum), and *fue* (flute made of bamboo). Stage assistants (*koken*) enter through the low stage door on the left and sit in the corner of the rear stage. From the same stage door, six or eight members of the chorus (*jiutai*) enter and sit on the border of the side stage. The secondary actor (*waki*), sometimes accompanied by a companion (*tsure*), enters through the passageway and states his name, intentions, and the places where he is going as he approaches the main stage. Finally the primary actor (*shite*) enters with or without his companion. All the performers are men, including those who play women's roles. Normally only the primary actor uses a mask.

Noh masks are carved of wood and painted. Mask carving is an art of its own. The noh mask appears expressionless by itself, but when used by an actor the same mask can take various expressions. Sometimes it appears to be weeping, and at other times smiling. The masks represent basic types of characters—holy old men, gods and demons, old men, spirits, men, and women. Masks of men and women are stylized faces of aristocrats of the Heian period. Some women's masks are of a beautiful young woman; some are the frightening face of a woman who became a demon out of anguish or jealousy.

The costumes are made of stiff silk cloth with rich application of brocade, damask, or embroidery. The large, loose garment with wide sleeves is donned above layers of silk undergarments. The gorgeous yet subdued color of the costumes gives a sense of refined luxury to the noh stage.

A full performance in a noh theater takes around six hours. Five noh plays are presented in any given program in an established sequence. The first drama is about the gods, the second about the ghosts of warriors, the third about a woman which is called *katsura-mono* (or wig play), the fourth about a mad person, and the fifth about a demon.

Many classical noh dramas express a Buddhist view of life, that is, the idea that life is transient. Typically they are composed in a theme as follows. A traveler visits a famous place; a villager appears, tells a story about the famous place, and then disappears after saying he is so-and-so in the story. As the traveler waits (there are many cases where he is sleeping), the villager appears again as his real self and tells about old times while dancing. With the coming of dawn the villager disappears, and the traveler awakens from his dream.

About 250 pieces of drama composed in the fourteenth and fifteenth centuries are performed today. The following are examples of famous dramas in the five categories presented in a noh program.

"Takasago" by Zeami (Seami). A traveling Shinto priest meets an ancient couple in a pine forest of Takasago; they turn out to be the spirits of ancient pine trees. This is one of the dramas about gods performed in the first part of a noh program.

"Yashima" by unknown author. A Buddhist priest visits Yashima in the Inland Sea, where the Heike and Genji clans fought their final battle. An old man making salt out of sea water there tells details of the battle, and at night, in the dream of the priest, he reveals himself as the ill-fated warrior Minamoto Yoshitsune. This is one of the warrior dramas performed in the second part of a noh program.

"Matsukaze" (Wind in the Pines) by Kan'ami. Two sisters who are dipping sea water at Suma beach appear to a Buddhist priest who seeks overnight lodging at a salt-maker's cottage. In the conversation in the moonlight, they reveal that they are the ghosts of Matsukaze and Murasame, once loved and then forsaken by the poet ARIWARA no Yukihira (818–893). In longing for her former lover, Matsukaze dons the court robes he once gave her and dances until the break of the dawn. This is an example of drama about a woman performed in part three.

"Sumidagawa" (River Sumida) by Kanze Motomasa (1394?–1432). A mad woman in grief over her kidnapped child travels a great distance from Kyoto to the eastern province (now Tokyo) in search of her boy. From the ferry man of the Sumida River, she learns that people gathered on the other side of the river are offering Buddhist prayers for her dead child, who was abandoned by slave dealers. She rushes into the crowd, strikes a gong, and chants prayers. The ghost of her child emerges from behind the burial mound and disappears at daybreak. This is a famous example of a mad-woman play.

"Momijigari" (Viewing Autumn Color) by KANZE Nobumitsu (1435–

1516). On a mountain slope in autumn, a beautiful woman of noble appearance and her lady attendants are enjoying a banquet under a maple tree covered with brilliant leaves. A nobleman who has been hunting on the mountain passes by and is invited to join the party. After drinking wine and watching the ladies dance, he falls asleep. Then the noble lady changes into a demon and attacks him. He struggles with a sword given by the mountain god and escapes. This is a play about demons presented in the fifth and last part of a noh program.

Kyogen

The stories of noh drama are serious and often tragic. Many express the pessimistic philosophy of Buddhism. To relieve the audience from tension, a short farce, or *kyogen* (literally, crazy words), is played in intervals. The language of noh is poetic and dignified, but in kyogen it is the colloquial speech of the Muromachi period. Kyogen takes the audience to a world of parody and comedy. Actors in kyogen ordinarily do not wear masks. When they do, the masks are comic versions of the noh masks.

In the modern era, new dramas have been written for noh and kyogen. Among them, works by novelist MISHIMA Yukio (1925–1970) are regarded as modern classics.

Puppet Theater *(Ningyo Joruri or Bunraku)*

Ningyo joruri is the generic term of puppet plays that are performed with the accompaniment of *joruri*, or narrative chanting. Joruri is a form of dramatic narrative chanting accompanied by *shamisen* (or *samisen*, a three-string instrument). Its origins go back to the tradition of blind Buddhist minstrels who recited legendary stories—especially the story of the downfall of the Heike (Taira) clan—while playing the *biwa* (lute). As to the origin of the term *joruri*, it is said that among the tales of the war between the Heike and Genji (Minamoto) clans in the twelfth century, the story of Princess Joruri who fell in love with Minamoto Yoshitsune, a tragic hero of the Genji clan, became very popular. As a result, dramatic chanting itself became identified as joruri.

In the seventeenth century, joruri was linked with puppet theater when a master joruri narrator in the Kyoto-Osaka area, TAKEMOTO Gidayu (1651–1714), teamed up with a dramatist, CHIKAMATSU Monzaemon (1653–1724), and produced masterpieces of puppet dramas. Of all puppet theaters of various local origins, the joruri of Kyoto-Osaka gained a nationwide reputation during the seventeenth and eighteenth centuries, and puppet theater accompanied by narrative chanting has come to be known as *ningyo* (puppet) *joruri*. Because of the enormous success of Takemoto Gidayu and his troupes, his school of joruri chanting came to be known as *Gidayu-bushi* (Gidayu tune) and became a leading school of joruri chanting. *Tokiwazu-bushi* and *Kiyomoto-bushi* are other major schools of chanting.

Ningyo joruri is also called *bunraku*. This is because Bunrakuza, the theater in Osaka dedicated to performances of ningyo joruri, became the most famous puppet theater in the nineteenth century.

The puppet play is performed by a narrator, an accompanist who plays *shamisen*, and puppeteers. All are male performers. The narrator and musicians, dressed in formal black costumes, are seated on an elevated platform on the side of the stage. The narrator recites all the parts of the puppets of both male and female characters, and he also gives explanatory comments. In earlier days, puppets were crudely made and their faces were expressionless. Later they were given elaborate features so that the puppeteers could move the puppets' mouth, eyes, and eyebrows, and the size of the puppets increased until they became about two-thirds that of their manipulators. In the earlier puppet theater, the audience could see only the puppets, which were either manipulated by strings from above or held from below by a puppeteer with his hands inside the puppets' bodies. Later, the puppets were manipulated by three puppeteers. The main operator moves the puppet's mouth, eyes, and right arm; the left operator works the left arm; the leg operator moves both legs. Needless to say, perfect coordination among the three is essential. In principle, the puppeteers wear black costumes and their faces are covered with black hoods to give the illusion that the puppets are acting by themselves. In puppet theater today, a team of three puppeteers clad in bright or somber costumes stands beside each puppet. Still, the audience is not supposed to see them and should concentrate only on the puppets.

The heads of the puppets are realistic representations of ordinary people. This is in contrast to the noh masks, which are subtle and symbolic representations of noble men and women, or ghosts. The contrast reflects the fact that puppet theater grew up among commoners, especially townsmen in the commercial centers of the Osaka area, whereas noh was patronized by the warrior rulers throughout the feudal age.

The plays written by CHIKAMATSU Monzaemon remain the greatest classic masterpieces of early modern Japan, and Chikamatsu is often referred to as the Japanese Shakespeare. He was born in a minor samurai family in the province of Echizen (present-day Fukui prefecture). The family moved to Kyoto when he was in his teens, and he served for some years as a page to a noble family. After sojourning for a while, he began to write drama under the stage name Chikamatsu. Perhaps his background and early experiences inspired his masterpieces not only about the everyday life of townsmen but also about events involving the ruling elite. In cooperation with TAKEMOTO Gidayu, the joruri chanter, and SAKATA Tojuro (1647–1709), a great kabuki actor in Osaka who had the reputation of being the equal of ICHIKAWA Danjuro I of Edo, Chikamatsu produced numerous masterpieces, including "The Love Suicide at Amijima," "The Love Suicide at Sonezaki," and "The Battle of Coxinga." The most successful play by Chikamatsu in his own time was "The Battle of Coxinga," an imaginary story based on historical events at the time of the Manchu conquest of China in the seventeenth century. It is a story of Japanese heroes who went to China to join the Chinese loyalists attempting to preserve the Ming Dynasty. Puppets could create spectacular scenes of fighting against a tiger and flying across mountain peaks riding on clouds. Also popular were domestic tragedies that portrayed men and women of the middle and lower classes, most dramatically represented by merchants, store clerks, and house servants who fall in love with prostitutes in pleasure quarters and get into serious trouble.

Kabuki

Kabuki was the most popular stage entertainment for commoners throughout the Tokugawa (Edo) period. It began in the early seventeenth century as a kind of variety show highlighting dancing and music performed by itinerant entertainers. It developed into a well-defined dramatic theater by taking in various elements from pre-existing theaters. From *kyogen*, it borrowed the style of dialogue; from *noh*, it borrowed plot, scenic stage design, gorgeous costumes, and graceful movement; from puppet theater, it borrowed narrative elements and music. Kabuki theater combines on one stage a drama with stylized acting and dialogues, dance, chanting of lyrical narratives with accompaniment by musical instruments, and acrobatic feats.

The stage of kabuki theater is picturesque. Spectacular scenes are created by the scenic setting, brilliant costumes, wigs, and special makeup for various types of characters—especially the strikingly bold makeup called *kumadori* for muscular-type characters in *aragoto* (rough play).

To signal the beginning of the performance, wooden clappers sound. Then the draw curtain with broad black, green, and orange stripes opens from stage right to stage left accompanied by more striking of wooden clappers. *Kamite* (stage left), the place of honor, is occupied by characters of high rank, their messengers, and honored guests. *Shimote* (stage right) is occupied by

characters of low rank and members of a household. The performers of narrative music who chant *nagauta* (literally, "long music"), *tokiwazu-bushi*, or *kiyomoto-bushi*, and the players of musical instruments for the *hayashi* ensemble, are dressed in formal black costumes and seated on an elevated platform on stage. They are regarded as equals with the actors as artists. A band of musicians who play background music and create sound effects are located behind the black screen on the back of the *shimote* and are not visible to the audience.

To enhance the visual effect, ingenious stage mechanisms have been devised, including revolving stages that make quick scene changes possible. *Hanamichi* (literally, "flower path"), a runway extended from the stage, passes through the audience to the back of the theater. It serves as a secondary stage as well as the passage for the actors to enter and exit. These devices became more elaborate during the eighteenth century to delight the audience, which expected more and more spectacular entertainment.

The patrons of kabuki in Tokugawa Japan were merchants, artisans, and all other sorts of townsmen, and they demanded exciting entertainment. To satisfy them it was more important to stage spectacular scenes than to present a well-developed theme. As a result, the plot became no more than an excuse to create various scenes as background for the choreographed performance. Typically each scene of kabuki is an anecdotal episode with its own build-up and resolution. A series of scenes is linked together to make up a whole play.

In its formative years the major theaters of kabuki were located in the two major cultural centers of Japan, namely, the Kyoto-Osaka area (referred to as *kamigata*) and Edo (Tokyo). Later kabuki gained greater popularity in Edo. Today kabuki is performed at the Kabukiza (Kabuki Theater, opened in 1889) and the Kokuritsu Gekijo (National Theater, built in Tokyo in 1966). Formerly the performance of a complete kabuki play could be an all-day affair. Today, the average length of a performance is about five hours including intermissions.

All actors on the kabuki stage, including those who perform women's characters, are men. This has been the tradition since 1629 when the Tokugawa authorities banned women entertainers on stage. The authorities, alarmed by the rising interest in male prostitution, also forbade kabuki performed by young men who had not yet reached majority (in those days, age 15). Since then, the role of female impersonator (*onnagata*) developed as an integral element of the kabuki theater. Actors who specialize in *onnagata* go through years of discipline and training to achieve the embodiment of idealized femininity. Ordinarily, actors specialize either in men's or women's roles, and only exceptionally versatile actors play all sorts of character types of both sexes.

Each actor belongs to an acting family by whose name he is identified. Ideally an actor is born into the family and trained under the head of the family; however, some actors are adopted by established professional families. When an actor is recognized as the successor to the leading actor of the family, he is allowed to inherit the name of his predecessor. This event does not only occur when he receives the final name; an actor receives different junior names at each step in his professional development. The formal ceremony followed by a public announcement on stage still remains an important event in an actor's career, although today he is hired by a theatrical enterprise and receives a salary. One of the great names, such as Ichikawa Danjuro, has been perpetuated for generations. In this family, Danjuro XI (i.e., the eleventh-generation ICHIKAWA Danjuro, 1909–1965) was a famous actor. Among leading actors today are the following: ICHIKAWA Ennosuke II (1939–), MATSUMOTO Koshiro (1942–), NAKAMURA Kichiemon II (1944–), BANDO Tamasaburo (1950–), ICHIKAWA Ebizo X (1951–), ONOE Tatsunosuke (1951–), NAKAMURA Kankuro V (1955–), KATAOKA Nizaemon, ONOE Kikunosuke, and ICHIKAWA Shinnosuke. Versatile actors nowadays perform not only in kabuki theater but also in Shakespearean and other modern drama, as well as in films and television. Matsumoto Koshiro, for example, acted in the modern musical "The King and I," which was performed not only in Japan but also in London.

The style of acting in kabuki plays is highly formalized. For various types of characters numerous patterns of stylized gesture, *kata* (form), are created. For example, to cut a *mie* (striking an attitude), the actor momentarily pauses to emphasize a high point in a scene, assumes a mighty pose, and glares defiantly often with eyes crossed. The *tate* (stylized fighting) is a skillfully choreographed series of spectacular movements representing combat; it is performed either by an individual or by a group of actors. Formalized patterns are effective in creating larger-than-life situations. A special sound effect made by wooden clappers, *tsuke* (accompaniment to action), enhances actions such as stamping on the ground or clashing sword blades in a duel. The man who does the *tsuke* in the wings closely watches the action in progress, holding the clappers ready to hit the sound-board on the floor.

In the spoken lines of a play, a 7–5 syllabic pattern (similar to that of classical poetry) with distinct rhythm and tempo is characteristic of kabuki. Extremely stylized speeches of great length give opportunities for actors to show off their elocutionary skill. In either monologues or dialogues, formalized speeches are used to create powerful effects—especially in plays about historic heroes. Informal colloquial forms are used in plays about ordinary people's everyday life. In either case, the language used in kabuki is a semi-classic style reflecting the formal and colloquial expressions of the Tokugawa period. For Japanese audiences today, it is not easy to follow the lines in kabuki without knowing classical Japanese. To attract larger audiences, more and more contemporary language is being incorporated into kabuki.

Stage assistants (*kurogo*) wear entirely black costumes. They assist the actors on stage, not only by handling the props actors use in performance but also—and most essential—by helping them change costumes (turning them inside out) when they suddenly transform into different characters. The feat of *hayagawari* (quick change) takes place on stage while the actor is continuously dancing or acting.

Types and Themes of Kabuki Plays

Kabuki that consists mainly of dancing or pantomimic actions is categorized as *shosa-goto* (action-centered piece). For example, "Kyoganoko Musume Dojoji" (Dancing Maiden at the Dojoji Temple) is based on a story about Kiyohime's unrequited love for Anchin, a monk of the Dojoji temple. At the dedication of a new bell at the temple, a beautiful maiden appears and begs to be allowed to dedicate her dance on the occasion. After a series of passionate dances she jumps into the bell and reappears as a serpent, a true form of Kiyohime. "Shakkyo" (Stone Bridge), another popular piece in this category, was developed from a *kyogen*. Other types of kabuki are dramas. Among them, *jidai-mono* (historical pieces) feature historical events or heroes from the past (i.e., before the Tokugawa period). Popular plays in this category include stories of court nobles; however, a much greater number of plays are based on legendary stories about warrior heroes. In particular, stories about Minamoto no Yoshitsune (1159–1189) inspired many dramas. Events during the Tokugawa era were dramatized as taking place in the historical past by setting the background in the earlier period. Dramas categorized as *sewa-mono* (contemporary piece) feature all sorts of heroes among commoners. Sensational events, such as love suicide, were favorite subjects in this category.

The major themes of kabuki of all types reflected the accepted values of Tokugawa society. These included reward to the good and punishment to the evil, loyalty to the lord, patriotism, and conflict between one's social obligations and personal feelings.

Playwrights of Kabuki

Many dramas written by Chikamatsu Monzaemon (1653–1724; see previous section on Puppet Theater) and other successful plays written for puppet theater were adapted for kabuki theater. In the formative years of kabuki, however, play writing was the performers' domain. The actors not only created various patterns of acting but also devised plot and dialogue. As an outstanding example, ICHIKAWA Danjuro I (1660–1704), who made his debut on the stage of Nakamuraza theater in Edo, created a distinguished style of acting to represent a masculine character. An extraordinarily talented performer and at the same time a dramatist, he contributed a great deal to elevate kabuki to the rank of mature drama. His successor, ICHIKAWA Danjuro II (1688–1758), also wrote one of the most popular plays, "Sukeroku yukari no Edozakura" (Sukeroku's Cherry Trees in Edo), and performed the leading role in it. Later generations of actors in the same acting family maintained the style of performance set by their predecessors and, at the same time, added individual flavor to the family tradition. Patrons came to the theater primarily to see their favorite actors perform. For them, plot was secondary.

Among distinguished actor-playwrights, NAMIKI Shozo I (1730–1773) wrote and performed kabuki in Osaka, and he is famous for devising the revolving stage. He studied under NAMIKI Sosuke (1695–1751), a *joruri* writer, who wrote the most popular puppet plays throughout the ages, such as "Kanadehon chushingura" (The Treasury of Loyal Retainers), "Sugawara denju tenarai kagami" (The Secret Instructions in Calligraphy Transmitted in the Sugawara Family), and "Yoshitsune sembonzakura" (Yoshitsune and One Thousand Cherry Trees). Among other distinguished actor-writers, there were NAMIKI Gohei I (1747–1808), who moved from Osaka to Edo, and TSURUYA Namboku IV (1755–1829). SAKURADA Jisuke I (1734–1806) wrote famous dramas including "Gohiiki kanjincho" (The Subscription List) in cooperation with actors Matsumoto Koshiro IV and Ichikawa Danjuro V. KAWATAKE Mokuami (1816–1893), who was originally a playwright of *kyogen*, was active through the early Meiji era writing popular kabuki plays. His most successful play was "Tokaido Yotsuya kaidan" (Ghost Story of Yotsuya on Tokaido Highway), which has been performed not only at kabuki theaters but also as versions of movies and television dramas. He is known as the first kabuki playwright whose works were printed and sold to the public.

As a part of a new literary movement in the late nineteenth and early twentieth centuries, writers of modern literature began to participate in creating kabuki drama. At the same time, the kabuki theater began to produce plays written by "outsiders" who were not professionally affiliated with the theater. TSUBOUCHI Shoyo (1859–1935), who led the reform movement and translated the entire plays of Shakespeare, wrote kabuki dramas too. Among those who joined his movement were OKAMOTO Kido (1872–1939), MAMIYA Seika (1878–1948), and KUBOTA Mantaro (1889–1963). Heavily influenced by modern European drama, these writers' plays were called *shin-kabuki* (new kabuki) to distinguish them from the traditional kabuki. Most new kabuki eliminated longstanding conventions such as background music played on traditional instruments. Some even adopted modern Western costume and used women actresses instead of *onnagata*. These plays did not gain popularity and ended as experiments; however, they served as important bridges between traditional and modern theater.

The most recent experiment in kabuki is "super kabuki," the work of accomplished kabuki performer Ichikawa Ennosuke II (1939–   ). Super kabuki makes full use of age-tested techniques in the kabuki tradition to produce dramas with new themes and contents appealing to the modern audience. In 1986 Ichikawa produced "Yamato Takeru," a drama about a legendary hero of the Divine Age in the *Kojiki* (the oldest written history of Japan) with the scenario written by UMEHARA Takeshi. By 1997 he had produced five more super kabuki written by Umehara on ancient history and by YOKOUCHI Kensuke, who wrote *sewa-mono* type based on old stories and folklore. Yet the mainstream of kabuki today involves performance of classical dramas, including those written in the early twentieth century featuring people who lived during the Tokugawa period.

Music

Traditional Japanese music before the introduction of Western music in the mid-nineteenth century is categorized as *hogaku*. It is regarded as a precious cultural asset, and the most distinguished masters of every genre of traditional music are officially designated as the "holders of important cultural property." They are more commonly known as "living national treasures." The most prestigious academy of music and fine arts, Tokyo Geijutsu Daigaku (Tokyo University of Fine Arts), has a division of hogaku. Only those who have attained the highest level of mastery in fine arts or performing arts are admitted to this school.

Ordinary people who want to learn traditional music must become students of private teachers (in the same manner as becoming a disciple of a master of tea ceremony or flower arrangement). Until the 1950s, well-to-do families sent their daughters to private teachers for lessons in traditional instruments or Japanese dance. Most teachers were women who gave lessons at their home. Such training was regarded as desirable for preparing young women for a good marriage, because they would learn not only traditional art but—more important—manners and etiquette under the precepts of traditional performing art. Nowadays children are too busy to take lessons in traditional arts. They would rather study piano or violin if they can find time after cram courses for entrance exams to higher-level schools.

Traditional folk songs (*min'yo*) are regarded as an important cultural legacy and are classified as hogaku. Every region of the country used to have its own folk songs sung in local dialect. Some of these are well known nationwide and sung by all. "Kiso-bushi" (Song of Kiso) of central Japan and "Itsuki no komoriuta" (Lullaby of Itsuki) of Kumamoto in Kyushu are familiar examples. More recent popular songs categorized as *enka* or *kayokyoku* are usually not treated as hogaku, even though they were originally based on folk songs. This is because the popular songs of postwar Japan were not considered deserving of inclusion in the category of hogaku. The most popular songs in postwar Japan were sung by MISORA Hibari (1937–1989), who started her career as a child singer and performed in movies. She was dubbed "the queen of *enka*" and has been remembered as a national hero who represented the early postwar generation. Most songs of this genre are sentimental and express traditional values of common folks.

For entertainment at private banquets at *ryotei* (high-class Japanese restaurants), music on traditional instruments is often performed. This is a continuation of the townsmen culture of the Tokugawa period when *geisha* (courtesans) entertained the restaurant patrons in pleasure quarters. Today a very small number of *geisha* are left.

In Japan, when a group of people have a banquet for recreation, they are likely to entertain each other by singing for the group. It is a well-established custom for companies to sponsor overnight group trips for the employees. At the hotel when they have a banquet in a large *tatami* (straw mat) room, everyone is urged to perform something for entertainment. To demonstrate their talent in music on such an occasion, some people take lessons in Japanese music. Nowadays, however, *karaoke* (literally, "empty orchestra," i.e. accompaniment orchestra without song) has pre-empted the need for lessons in classical instruments.

Among the traditional instruments *koto, shamisen,* and *shakuhachi* are still popular, and they are often played as an ensemble. *Koto* is a six-foot-long, thirteen-string zither with sound box made of paulownia wood. It is laid flat on the tatami floor and played with plectrums (picks). It has a harp-like tone and was a favorite instrument of noble men and women of the Heian Court. It has long been regarded as the most suitable instrument for solo or chamber ensembles at mansions of high taste. In the early twentieth century, MIYAGI Michio composed much modern koto music. "Haru no umi" (Spring Sea) for *koto* and *shakuhachi* (later, the *shakuhachi* part was arranged for violin) is a famous piece composed by Miyagi.

Shamisen (also called *samisen* or *sangen*) is a three-stringed plucked lute with a sound box covered with parchment. It is used primarily as an accompaniment instrument for chanting at kabuki and puppet theater as well as for private entertainment in a small room.

Shakuhachi is an end-blown bamboo flute. It does not have a reed and requires skill to play. It is usually played by men, following the tradition of wandering Buddhist monks and former samurai during the medieval ages. There are other kinds and sizes of flutes, all made of bamboo.

Among other traditional instruments are *biwa* (lute with four strings), *kotsuzumi* (small hand drums), *otsuzumi* (big hand drum), and *taiko* (drum). *Taiko* and bamboo flute were used in *matsuri bayashi*, or ensemble music, for festivals and *bon odori*, evening outdoor dances at the mid-summer festivals. Every local community used to hold summer festivals and *bon odori*, which were participated in by men and women wearing *yukata* (summer cotton *kimono*.) This is one of the vanishing customs of Japan. Nowadays, communities cannot find young men who are interested in practicing traditional flute or drum. Recorded music and loudspeakers seem to have replaced live music performed by local people.

Almost all kinds of modern Western music are performed in Japan today. Most concert halls feature Western music, as do recording companies and radio and television programs. This includes the most up-to-date popular music by Japanese and foreign composers. The standard curriculum of music education in secondary schools is exclusively Western music. When Japan developed as a modern nation in the mid-nineteenth century, the government and the public placed great emphasis on catching up with modern world civilization centered on the West. Music was no exception. Moreover, many young people were genuinely attracted to European music and became dedicated students in Europe. As a result, there are world-class performers among Japanese musicians.

The well-known Suzuki method of music education, which is based on the belief that children can learn music in the same way as they learn language, was started by SUZUKI Shin'ichi (1898–1998). He was the son of a violin maker in Nagoya and studied music in Berlin before World War II, when Albert Einstein lived there and also played the violin. After returning to Japan, Suzuki had an active career as a performer and a teacher. In 1946 he started a private music academy to teach children in the city of Matsumoto in Nagano prefecture, where the 1998 Winter Olympic Games were held.

For the opening ceremony of the Olympic Games in Nagano in 1998, another internationally renowned musician from Japan, OZAWA Seiji of the Boston Symphony Orchestra, conducted his orchestra and chorus in the Nagano Culture Center Hall. With the help of television screens, he simultaneously conducted the orchestras and choruses of five major cities in the five continents of the globe in performing Beethoven's Ninth Symphony.

Not only in performing Western music but also in composing music for Western orchestras, Japanese musicians have made significant contributions. Among Japanese composers trained in Europe, TAKEMITSU Toru and MAYUZUMI Toshiro, both of whom passed away in 1997, were well known for their compositions using elements of the Japanese musical tradition.

FINE ARTS

Painting

Just as many other traditional arts, Japanese painting was influenced by Chinese art brought to Japan during the ancient and medieval ages. Buddhist paintings were among the earliest. Because Japanese painters followed the Chinese tradition, it takes specialists to distinguish between most Chinese and Japanese paintings. However, the Japanese artists created some distinctively Japanese styles.

Yamato-e (Japanese-style painting) is a Japanese modification of Chinese landscape painting. In this category, scroll painting is the best known.

Emakimono (picture scrolls) appeared in the late Heian period. Each long scroll, about one foot in width, narrates a story with pictures and explanatory text in chronological order. *The Tale of Genji* scrolls and Ban Dainagon scrolls are among the most famous of this kind.

Shoheiga (paintings on screens and sliding doors) developed primarily as decorative paintings for temples and castles of feudal lords in the sixteenth century. Paintings in bold designs are executed on gold-foil background, reflecting the sumptuous taste of the new warrior-elite of the time. The favorite subjects are landscapes, ferocious animals (especially tigers), dragons, and demon-like images of the spirits of thunder and storm. KANO Eitoku (1543–1590), the master of this genre, established the influential Kano school of painting. Painters of this school were patronized by the Tokugawa rulers and enjoyed power and prestige.

Shodo (Calligraphy)

The tradition of writing with brush and black ink has as long a history as the writing system in Japan, since brush was the only instrument for writing on paper until the Western-style pen was introduced in the modern age. Brush writing requires discipline. One's penmanship (or brushmanship) was always regarded as an important reflection of one's personality, because the characters one writes were believed to express one's personal character.

Brush writing has been an important part of primary school education. In addition to lessons at school, many children take private lessons in calligraphy after school. The tradition of *kakizome* on January 2, the first writing of the new year, is still observed today. Traditionally, this day was the first day of practicing all sorts of art.

Calligraphy as a form of creative art gave rise to various styles, some that are very much like abstract painting. Just as in many other forms of traditional art, calligraphy generated numerous schools centering around renowned masters. National organizations of calligraphers organize annual exhibits.

Kogei (Handicraft Art)

Skilled artisans of traditional handicrafts are held in high esteem in Japan. Today, the government recognizes distinguished artisans as the holders of important cultural property and pays them a lifetime annual stipend. They are generally known as *ningen kokuho* (living national treasures). As of 1998, there are 99 of them, of whom 50 are performing artists and 49 are masters of various kinds of handicraft art. They are mostly accomplished elderly artists. The youngest among the *ningen kokuho* is a 59-year-old musician who plays *taiko* (drum) for noh drama.

Ceramics (Toki and Jiki)

The earliest known potteries have been discovered in the sites of the Jomon culture of 12,000 years ago. These were used for storing and cooking food and for making symbolic figurines that were presumably used in religious rituals. Later, advanced technology in pottery making—such as use of the potters' wheel, glazing, and *noborigama* (climbing kiln)—was brought from China through Korea. Kilns were developed in various localities in Japan, and potteries with local characteristics were marketed throughout the country. The finest craftsmanship was dedicated to making tea bowls for the tea ceremony.

Arita were, also known as Imari, of Saga prefecture in Kyushu is characterized by the application of polychrome enamels on cobalt or milk-white underglaze. The technique was developed by SAKAIDA Kakiemon, who lived in Arita in the early Tokugawa period. The art and technique have been handed down in his family to this day.

Karatsu ware is an older earthen ware made in Karatsu, Saga prefecture, on the northern shore of Kyushu. Kutani ware of Ishikawa prefecture competes with Arita ware in rich decorative pattern. In Kyoto, decorated earthen ware or stone ware known as Kyoyaki was developed by artisans such as OGATA Kenzan (1666–1743). Kilns in Seto in Aichi prefecture have produced a large quantity of porcelain for everyday use. *Seto-mono* (Seto ware) has become a generic name for everyday porcelain. Many other famous kilns in central and western parts of Honshu, such as Mino, Bizen, Tamba, Shigaraki, and Hagi, produce nationally famous ceramic ware. In northeastern Honshu, Mashiko ware of folksy taste is produced.

Lacquer Ware (Shikki)

Sometimes called Japan ware (in contrast to China ware, which means ceramics), *shikki* includes wooden containers, utensils, or furniture coated with *urushi* (lacquer) from the Japanese lacquer tree. Leather, paper, porcelain, and metal can also be coated with urushi. Nowadays plastic material is used in place of wood. Various types of lacquer ware are identified by place name. For example, Wajima ware is produced in Wajima, Ishikawa prefecture.

Japanese Sword (Nihonto)

There are over two hundred schools of Japanese swordsmith artists, each with its own characteristics of craftsmanship.

Other Handicraft Arts

Among other handicrafts that are officially recognized as important cultural property are *senshoku* (dyeing and weaving), *noh-men* (noh mask) making, and paper making.

IKEBANA (FLOWER ARRANGEMENT)

Now internationally known, *ikebana* is formally called *kado* (the way of flower). It developed along with tea ceremony and other Zen art during the Muromachi period. In this tradition, flowers are arranged not merely for the sake of decoration but rather as a form of creative art. Like *haiku* (short poems in 17 syllables), sensibility to the changes of four seasons is an important element in ikebana. Also, like the Zen garden, a pot of arranged flowers is supposed to symbolize a landscape and even to express the spirit of the universe. The three main branches in the traditional form of arrangement are called "heaven," "earth," and "man."

Various styles of flower arrangement developed throughout the ages. The major styles used today are as follows:

- *Rikka* (standing, or vertical style, flowers): aims at realizing a symbolic representation of landscape. It has the most formal and structured pattern, involving the positioning of seven (later, nine) main branches as the core of its structure. Its dignified appearance makes it suitable to be placed in the *tokonoma* (decorative alcove) for most formal ceremonial occasions.
- *Seika* or *Shoka* (living flowers): less formal than *rikka* but still dignified. Its emphasis is on expressing the way flowers grow on earth. The vase is considered to represent the earth. Flowers are arranged in a triangle structure around primary (*shin*), secondary (*soe*), and tertiary (*tai*) branches.
- *Nageire* (thrown-in flowers): free-style but still suitable to be placed in *tokonoma*. The flowers are put in a tall vase and allowed to fall naturally. Some vases are made for hanging on a pillar.
- *Moribana* (piled-up flowers): a modern variation devised in the early twentieth century to accommodate small flowers, especially those of European origin. They are arranged in low, shallow containers.
- *Flower Designing*: a totally free style that disregards traditional forms of ikebana.

The teachers of flower arrangement, like those of tea ceremony, dance, painting, or any other traditional Japanese arts, are supposed to maintain the secret tradition handed down in the family of their teachers. After studying under a mentor for many years, a disciple is allowed to learn the secret technique step by step and is finally certified as a teacher. In fact, teacher and disciples form a hierarchical group similar to that of the traditional family (*ie*) system, and like the *ie*, students can form branch groups. This is known as the *iemoto* system, which is the basis of numerous schools of ikebana.

It is said that there are over two thousand schools of ikebana. The largest among them is the Ikenobo school, which was founded during the Muromachi period. The next largest, the Ohara school, was established in the early twentieth century. The Sogetsu school is an avant-garde school founded by TESHIGAHARA Sofu (1906–1979). The flower arrangements of this school and other avant-garde schools incorporate all sorts of natural and artificial material, and some of them resemble modern sculpture.

Flower arrangement has been one of the arts for finishing school for young women. Even for working women, it is a favorite after-work activity. Those who continue to study, and pay fees and tuition to their teachers and schools, can be certified as teachers to start their own schools at home. Most teachers of flower arrangement are married women who teach at home or at local cultural centers.

BONSAI

Bonsai literally means potted and trained miniature trees or plants. They are made to look like they are growing in nature. The art of growing and shaping such trees or plants is also referred to as *bonsai*. The concept and technique of bonsai originated in China and were transmitted to Japan around the thirteenth century along with landscape painting and other elements of Zen culture.

Bonsai can be made from any ordinary trees or plants; however, the most favored kinds in Japan are pine trees, plums, and bamboos. Japanese maples are also very common. They are grown outdoors but are displayed inside as art pieces for special occasions.

To start a bonsai, seeds or naturally grown young trees can be used. The height of a completed bonsai ranges from two inches to three feet. Various techniques are used to achieve the desired sizes and aesthetically pleasing shapes. There are specific methods for pruning branches and roots, pinching off new growth, and wiring branches and trunks. Special tools, pots, and miniature garden rocks are manufactured for bonsai. The trees can be shaped in various ways to satisfy the artistic taste of any cultivator. Regardless of their ultimate shape, the trees must look as though they grew naturally. Any traces of artificial intervention must be unnoticeable.

A unique aesthetic value of bonsai is expressed through the vigor, shape, and structure of the plant. Like flower arrangement, bonsai is meant to express "heaven and earth" (i.e., the universe) in one container. The tree must always be positioned off-center in its container, and the branches must develop in asymmetric patterns. If the tree has a pair of branches spreading from the two sides of the tree at the same height, one must be cut off to avoid symmetry. A bonsai can be shaped in various ways to convey scenic beauty in nature, such as an upright tree, a tree hanging down from a cliff toward a gorge, or a tree whose root clings to rocks instead of being grounded in the earth.

Healthy and well-maintained bonsai can live for decades or even over a century. Aged bonsai are more respected than younger ones and are handed down from generation to generation within a family.

CHANOYU OR SADO (TEA CEREMONY)

Chanoyu, known as "tea ceremony" in the Western world, is a form of art centering on serving and drinking tea. It is considered a refined art of entertainment for elegant social gatherings emphasizing the appreciation of aesthetic taste. It encompasses various arts and crafts such as ceramics for tea bowls, paintings and calligraphy for the hanging scrolls that decorate tea rooms, flower arrangement, architecture, and landscape gardening, as well as proper behavior and conversation.

Tea used for chanoyu is *mattcha* (finely ground green tea powder) with a bitter taste. To serve a bowl of tea properly, one must follow a strict set of rules. To drink a bowl of tea, the same kind of code of behavior must be followed by the guests. To make a bowl of tea, a scoop or two of tea powder (in a thin bamboo scoop) is placed in a tea bowl, in which hot water heated in a cast-iron tea kettle on the sunken hearth in the tea room is poured with a small bamboo ladle. The amount of water is not to exceed about a quarter of the capacity of the tea bowl. A delicate bamboo whisk is used to mix the tea briskly. This produces a fine foam on the surface of tea.

The host prepares the tea in the presence of the guest(s) following a set of rules of conduct handed down in each school of tea masters. There are meticulous rules about how to walk in the tea room, sit down, greet each other, hold the tea cup, handle each of the utensils, pour water into the tea cup, and so on. The entire procedure takes place in silence. In fact, making tea is almost like performing a choreographed act, and the movement of a tea master is indeed graceful. When the tea is offered, the guest bows, holds the bowl with both hands, takes a sip, and drinks up the rest of the tea all at once. In the past, there was a type of group tea drinking in which a number of guests seated in a circle passed around a single tea bowl, taking a sip one after another. This custom is no longer followed, even at outdoor tea parties with many guests.

After drinking tea, the guest is expected to carefully examine and praise the artistic quality of the tea bowl and utensils used for making the tea, such as the caddy in which the tea powder is stored, the bamboo tea scoop, the iron kettle that sounds like gusts of wind passing though a pine grove when the water begins to boil, or even the charcoal in the hearth. Then the guest is supposed to pay close attention to the hanging scroll and flower arrange-

Tea ceremony room in garden. Courtesy of Noriko Kamachi.

ment in the tea room, expressing admiration for each of them. Displaying one's art collection by selecting the best-suited tea bowls and utensils as well as decorating the tea room for the particular occasion has been an important part of tea gatherings since the very beginning of the tradition.

The tea ceremony room (*chashitsu*) is regarded as a sanctuary from everyday life. The ideal room is small enough for four and a half *tatami* mats, with one small window open to the garden. The entranceway for guests, called *nijiriguchi* (crawling-in entrance), should be barely large enough for a person to crawl in on the knees. The narrow passage is intended to create a separate realm from the outside world of everyday life. A tea ceremony room is an expression of aesthetic taste that prefers restrained beauty, refined simplicity, and voluntary pursuit of material deprivation. Such taste is expressed in the words *sabi* (derived from "loneliness") and *wabi* (another word for "loneliness"), and many philosophical treatises have been written on their profound meanings.

The tea culture is historically associated with Zen Buddhism and thus has been regarded as a part of Zen culture. Although tea drinking was known in Japan before the Heian period, the use of powdered tea was transmitted from China during the Kamakura period. Monk Eisai (1141–1215), who studied in China and became the founder of the Rinzai sect of Zen in Japan, not only brought powdered tea back from China but also wrote a book on tea drinking, *Kissa yojoki* (Tea Drinking for Health), recommending tea as beneficial to health. The followers of Zen used tea as both a medicine and a drink to stay awake during their seated meditation. Tea was also served at banquets held at the conclusion of religious ceremonies in Buddhist temples. The rules for handling tea developed in Zen monasteries.

Zen Buddhism attracted the samurai ruling elite, who found the disciplined lifestyle at the monasteries to their liking. As a result, Zen culture including tea drinking became an important part of the samurai elite culture. Also, tea drinking became fashionable among rich townsmen—especially the merchants of Sakai, the largest port city for international trade during the Kamakura and Muromachi periods when imports from China were highly valued. The merchants' wealth and connection with overseas traders enabled them to acquire Chinese porcelains, paintings, and other arts and crafts. For Sakai merchants, social gatherings for tea drinking were occasions to enhance their social and political influence. Display of their art works became an essential part of tea gatherings.

During the Muromachi period, tea gatherings became a symbol of the new wealth and culture of the military elite. The Ashikaga family, who founded the Muromachi *bakufu* in Kyoto, patronized Zen monasteries and Zen culture. Other military aristocrats did the same. Invitation to tea gatherings held by prestigious lords had important political significance.

In defining the rules of behavior and setting aesthetic standards for the tea culture, SEN no Rikyu (1522–1591) was the most crucial: he emphasized the aesthetic aspects of *wabi* and *sabi*, and he created various devices including the *nijiriguchi*, the small entrance to the tea room from the garden, as part of the design of the tea room. Rikyu was born in a merchant family in Sakai and distinguished himself as a tea practitioner. He served ODA Nobunaga, then TOYOTOMI Hideyoshi, as curator of their art collections, tea master, and even political confidant. His position as leading tea master enabled him to become involved in politics among the warrior elite, which eventually caused his downfall and death by forced suicide. His followers carried on his tradition of tea and maintained his reputation as a model tea master. Today the three branches of the Sen family—namely, Omote Senke, Ura Senke, and Mushakoji Senke—are leading authorities in the world of tea. Moreover, the Sen family is an outstanding example of the survival of the *iemoto* (family headship) system that developed during the feudal era in various arts and crafts.

When the feudal era came to a close in the mid-nineteenth century, the tea culture was temporarily overshadowed by the national zeal for westernization. However, the families of tea masters adapted to the demands of modern age and succeeded in making the tea culture even more popular than ever. They encouraged women to participate in tea gatherings, which formerly were almost exclusively dominated by men. As a result, there are more women than men among tea masters in Japan today. In prewar Japan tea was introduced in the school curriculum, especially in girls' schools as the principal means to train students in etiquette and deportment. In the postwar period, training in tea was still regarded as essential preparation for women to be desirable brides. Today, lessons in the tea ceremony are popular at culture centers all over Japan.

5

Housing and Architecture

RESIDENTIAL ARCHITECTURE

Houses in Japan Today

"Japanese-style" houses with baked roof tiles, white plaster walls, wood panels, sliding doors, and a garden were the norm in middle-class neighborhoods in Japan to around the 1960s. Now they are rapidly disappearing. In their place, smaller houses with new concepts, new designs, and new building material are being constructed. Many old lots have been taken over by high-rise condominiums, a result of the economic boom of the 1960s and 1980s when soaring land prices forced middle-class families to settle with smaller lots. Traditional farmhouses in the countryside, which had remained essentially the same for many centuries, also have undergone substantial transformation in the past few decades. Farmers' houses nowadays have more modern facilities such as indoor plumbing, and they are not much different from those in urban suburbs.

New houses in urban areas are designed not only for economy of space and building cost but also to accommodate modern facilities such as air-conditioning (and even central heating for those who can afford it), as well as the need for security. A traditional house had many sliding doors opening to the outside that required a lot of work to lock up. The primary concerns about a house in the past were to get enough sunlight and to allow free flow of fresh air through the house. As people began to prefer newer designs and more cost-efficient building materials, houses in Japan began to appear more like those in European and North American cities. Despite their appearance, however, the interior design of Japanese houses is quite different from that of Europe and North America—not only because of limited space but also because of a relatively unchanging lifestyle. A typical middle-class house in Japan today is a practical combination of traditional Japanese concepts and modern Western style.

In the following section, characteristic elements of "traditional-style" houses in modern Japan are discussed. Readers are cautioned in advance, however, that very few people in Japan can afford to build a house in the traditional style today. Building materials for such houses are very expensive, and there are fewer carpenters with traditional skills. To see well-kept traditional houses, one must visit museums. There are still many old traditional-style houses remaining in cities, but they are rapidly disappearing. Nevertheless, certain traditional concepts are being resurrected by acclaimed modern architects, who creatively adapt the aesthetic elements of traditional Japanese houses to modern buildings equipped with modern conveniences.

The traditional Japanese house was built to accommodate the climate, which is characterized by long hot summers with plentiful rainfall and relatively mild winters. To cope with high humidity, the floor is raised off the ground and the interior is opened up to allow free flow of air across the house. Most inner partitions are made of removable sliding panels, such as *fusuma* (wood-framed sliding door covered with thick paper, often with landscape paintings on it) and *shoji* (wood-framed sliding door with lattice covered with translucent paper). The *amado* (storm doors) made of panel wood are also sliding doors, and they are closed at night. Outside the storm doors, *engawa* (a long, narrow veranda made of unfinished wood planks) is open to the garden. To protect the interior and the engawa, roofs have long overhangs.

Traditionally, the roofs of houses in urban areas were covered with tiles of baked clay, which have been replaced today with more economical and lighter synthetic tile. Roofs are supported by wooden posts that rest on foundation stones without being cemented so that when an earthquake occurs, the posts can slide off the foundation stones with little or no damage to the building. All joints in traditional buildings were mortised, tenoned, and pegged so that few or no nails were needed. The joinery of post and lintel formed the top of window or door frames. The standard distance between the posts was six feet, which became the unit of measurement for Japanese building. The walls are essentially bamboo lattices plastered with clay; they were not intended to sustain the weight of the roofs and other structural forces from the rest of the building, but simply to be barriers between the interior spaces. Diagonal support between columns was not an

Veranda and garden of a Japanese house. Courtesy of Horace Bristol/Corbis.

unknown concept but generally was not used. After the devastation of the 1995 earthquake in the Kobe area exposed the vulnerability of traditional houses, use of the diagonal has been promoted to reinforce the integrity of structures.

To build a house, it was essential to engage a carpenter (*daiku*) who would design the house in accordance with the requests of the patron and build it with apprentices and hired laborers. The basic parts of the building are prepared in the workshop, and in one day the columns are erected, the beams are placed, and the skeletal framework of the house is constructed. Nowadays, however, the more convenient way is to engage a construction company that sells prefabricated houses.

Around the house and the garden, walls made of shrubbery, concrete blocks, or other material shield the inside from the view of passers-by. At the opening of the wall facing the street, gate posts are erected. A visitor approaches the house through the gate (which is normally open during the daytime) and from outside the front entrance of the house, shouts *"gomen*

House gate. Courtesy of Noriko Kamachi.

kudasai" (Excuse me, please), unless there is a doorbell. Inside the front door is the *genkan* (entrance hall), which is partly dirt or a floor covered with tiles. Once the visitor is invited inside the house, he or she takes off his or her shoes before stepping up to the paneled floor. The host often offers slippers to walk through the hallway. When shown into a room covered with *tatami* (straw mat covered with woven surface), the visitor takes off the slippers before stepping into the room.

The rooms are laid out as multiples of floor mats (*tatami*). The size of a room is measured by the number of tatami covering the floor. The standard tatami is six feet by three feet, weighing about sixty pounds. The base of tatami is made of pressed straw of about two inches thick. Its surface is covered with a thin sheet made of rush. The border is bound by linen, cotton, or synthetic fabric. Nowadays, however, tatami is increasingly made of plastic material. Usually, the reception parlor (*zashiki*) is the largest tatami room in a house. The typical size zashiki in an old middle-class family house was between eight and twelve tatami. On one end of the zashiki is a raised floorboard called *tokonoma*. It is a special alcove and ceremonial focal point of the room. A scroll painting or calligraphy hangs on the wall behind it, and a flower arrangement or small sculpture sits on the floorboard. This is the space where special decorations are placed for major festivals such as New

Genkan: entrance hall of a house. Courtesy of Noriko Kamachi.

Years, Doll festival, Boy's festival, and Mid-Autumn Moon-Viewing festival. On the side of the tokonoma is a space for a decorative shelf (*chigai-dana*) where artistic objects are displayed. The *toko-bashira*, the beautiful large pillar between tokonoma and chigai-dana, is regarded as the most important pillar of the house, and the best timber is used for it. The place before the toko bashira is the seat of honor. Each tatami room usually has a built-in closet (*oshiire*) of one tatami size covered by sliding screen doors (*fusuma*). These screen doors are of equal height and width, and the ones between rooms can be easily removed to create a larger space.

To sit in a tatami room, a flat cushion called *zabuton* (literally, "seating futon") is used. When visiting someone's house, it is polite to wait to use the cushion until being offered. Also, when the host or other members of the family or other visitors come into the room, it is proper for the visitor to move off the zabuton to exchange greetings by kneeling directly on the tatami. The formal seating position on tatami is to sit on one's feet, keeping the knees together and maintaining the back upright. It takes some training to stay in this position for an extended time. It is permissible to excuse oneself and change to a more relaxed posture after the formal greeting is over. Once seated in a tatami room, however, one should never stand up until one leaves the room.

Tokonoma alcove: Japanese tea house. Courtesy of Patrick J. Young/ University of Michigan, Ann Arbor: Japanese Gallery.

Most new houses nowadays have only one or two tatami rooms, if any. If there are, they are used for bedrooms. Few houses have a formal reception parlor as the ritual center of the house. At the turn of the twentieth century, many well-to-do families added a European-style *osetsuma* (reception room). Carpet, sofa, coffee table, cupboard with wine glasses and coffee cups, and even a piano became new status symbols. Even now when the average middle-class house is very small, people still want a separate space for entertaining guests. The idea is that the formal space for guests and informal space for family need to be separated. This is very different from the American concept of friendliness. If ever invited to a Japanese house, visitors should not intrude into the kitchen or other family space.

The family room or living room, called *chanoma* (literally, "tea room"), is used as the dining room with everyone sitting on the tatami floor around the low table. In the winter time, this table is replaced with a *kotatsu*, a square framework covered with a quilt and equipped with an electric heating system for warming the space inside. A table top over the quilt makes a kotatsu function as a table. In the past when the heating system with thermostat was not available, the kotatsu's source of heat was a red-hot charcoal buried in ashes in a covered container or, preferably, in a sunken hearth. Between meals, the room is used for activities such as needlework, paperwork, knitting, or reading. At night the table can be folded up and the room used as a bedroom.

Tatami rooms used as bedrooms do not usually have any bed. A set of bedding—consisting of futon mattress and larger and softer futon for covering, sheets, and small pillow filled with buckwheat chaff or beans—is stored in the *oshiire* (closet) during the daytime and laid out on the tatami at night. On dry and sunny days, people air out their futons in the sun. Nowadays, many people use mattresses under the futons, but these mattresses can be folded in three parts and stored in the closet.

The bath room is usually separate from the toilet. A deep bathtub (formerly made of wood but now made of plastic or stainless steel) sits on the tiled floor with drainage. Before getting in the bathtub, one must rinse on the tiled floor. Washing with soap and shampoo also are done on the tiled floor. The bathtub is only for soaking and relaxing. The entire family uses the same bath water once it has been heated for the day. It takes a lot of time and expensive energy to fill the deep bathtub, and it is unthinkable to change the water for every individual. That's why everyone must be mindful not to dirty the bath water. (It used to be that the male family head always took the bath first. Women were the last. Nowadays bathing order is not an issue, because family size is smaller and fathers tend to stay late at work.)

Having bath facilities in each house and apartment is a luxury enjoyed by most Japanese people today; however, until only thirty years ago the average working person could not afford such a luxury. In those days, in every neighborhood there was a public bath house where people wearing wooden clogs used to go carrying towel and soap in a washing pan. Today, some public baths have modern facilities such as saunas and showers.

The Japanese custom of taking a hot bath at the end of the day, every day, has attracted attention on the part of foreign reporters. Many emphasize that it is a kind of religious ritual whereby the Japanese purify themselves. Indeed, there is some ritual element in bathing. Certain old families in the rural areas maintain the custom of bathing early in the morning on the first day of the new year before conducting the New Years ceremony. Bathing and abstinence (from meat and sexual contact) were the central elements of ritual purification in the Shinto religion. For ordinary people in everyday life, however, bathing at the end of the day is a practical matter. In the hot, humid summer, one wants to wash off the dirt and sweat of the day after coming home on a crowded commuter train. In winter, it is essential to warm up in a hot bath before going to bed. Houses in Japan usually do not have central heating, and for the sake of safety all space-heating equipment must be turned off at night.

The "Japanese-style" house of today is a development from the residential style of medieval samurai, known as the *shoin-zukuri* (studio-style, or study-alcove style), which developed during the Muromachi period between the fourteenth and sixteenth centuries. The most distinct characteristic of the studio-style house is that it is built around a *shoin* (studio) or main parlor for receiving visitors and conducting formal rituals. The interior design and decoration of shoin were modeled after the study built for priests in Zen monasteries. Its floor was covered wall-to-wall with tatami mat. It had a tokonoma alcove, a writing desk built into one wall, partition by sliding doors, and more sliding doors with translucent paper over the desk. The concept and design of *zashiki* in the later period was an outgrowth of the shoin style of architecture. The shoin must have a garden around it, providing protective space to secure serenity inside the house and a scene for contemplation in the studio.

The concept of shoin as the formal parlor of a house was an outgrowth of the *shinden-zukuri (shinden*-style, or main-hall style) architecture of the Heian period. (For *shinden-zukuri*, see the section "Gardens" later in this chapter.) A *shinden*-style mansion was constructed around the main hall, which was used by the head of the mansion for receiving honorable guests and conducting rituals. These mansions, however, had a large room with bare floor, and the space inside the building was divided by folding screens and removable partitions. Its doors were hinged on the beams and had to be lifted open, just like old-fashioned garage doors in America. Its thatched roofs were supported by large round columns. In contrast, the *shoin*-style houses had interior walls, sliding doors between square-cut posts, and tatami mats to cover the floors.

Out of the shoin-style architecture, *sukiya-zukuri* residential architecture developed in the early Tokugawa period. *Sukiya* meant "tea room." A free-style variation of the studio-style architecture, it is characterized by asymmetrical design and highly decorative elegance. Just as the studio-style, the *sukiya*-style design was primarily for the main parlor of a house; however, the design influenced the rest of the residential architecture.

For Japanese families, a single-family house with garden is the ideal. Nowadays, to realize their dream, most people who work in large cities have to settle with a small plot a great commuting distance from work, because of the population concentration in metropolitan areas and high land prices. The average floor space of new houses built in 1993 was 92 square meters (roughly

Tightly packed train during morning rush hour. Courtesy of Kyodo News.

920 square feet) nationwide and 62 square meters (about 620 square feet) in Tokyo. Per capita floor space (national average) in 1993 was 30.6 square meters, which is about one-half that of the United States (reported to be 59 square meters in 1993) but not much less than those of the European countries (39 square meters in Germany, 38 square meters in the United Kingdom, and 37 square meters in France).

The average cost of a single-family house in Tokyo in 1997 was 12.9 times the average annual income, and 9.5 times in Osaka. Average people in Japan must spend a higher proportion of their income on houses than their counterparts in Europe and the United States. In the early 1990s the average cost of a house in New York City was 2.9 times a person's average income; in Paris, 3.4 times; and in London, 6.9 times.[1] In Japan the higher cost of housing in the center of the city pushes commuters further into the distant areas. Living a great distance from work means commuting long hours in tightly packed commuter trains. In fact, trains during morning rush hours are so crowded that railway stations place extra personnel on the platforms to help passengers squeeze into already packed cars.

Traditional farmhouses in rural areas used to have thatched roofs. Inside the heavy panel doors at the front entrance was a large hall with dirt floor, used for storage and work space for various kinds of indoor activities such as weaving. The dirt floor continued all the way through the back door, where the kitchen was located. Stoves used firewood and dried straws. The family well was located either inside or outside the kitchen. Around the main building were the bath house, outhouse, shelters for farm tools and draft animals, and chicken coops. The interior of farmhouses had raised floors and tatami-covered rooms used as main parlor, drawing room, and bedroom.

In recent years rural farmhouses, especially those near the suburbs of large cities, have become more similar to urban houses. Farmers no longer thatch the roofs because it is more expensive than using roof tiles.

Multiple Dwellings

Multiple-unit dwellings are not new in Japan. Wood-frame, one-story row houses with shared bathroom facilities, called *nagaya*, were familiar sites in large cities during the Tokugawa period. Residents of *nagaya* were working people with humble means. Daily life in their community, poor but rich in a sense of humor, has been a favorite topic of traditional-style talk shows. In contrast, the Western-style apartment house, which first appeared in Tokyo after the great earthquake of 1923, symbolized modern progress, individualism, and a high level of convenience.

During the years following the Pacific War, cities in Japan (especially Tokyo, which was heavily bombed toward the end of the war) suffered an acute housing shortage. To ameliorate the problem, the government created a nonprofit public developer, Japan Housing Corporation, in 1955. It constructed a large number of concrete-reinforced multi-story apartment buildings and housing projects, known as *danchi*, comprised of rows of apartment buildings.

Thereafter, the layout of *danchi* apartments became the model for apartments in Japan. The concept of the dining-kitchen (popularly referred to as DK), a space of about 8 square meters (86 sq. feet), which is used for both cooking and dining, was one of the innovations for the danchi apartments. The layout of the most popular apartment for a couple with one child was the so-called 2LDK, which included two living rooms (used for bedrooms at night, most likely one with six tatami mats and the other with 4.5 tatami mats), a dining-kitchen, toilet room, bath room, and small entrance space for taking off and storing shoes. Every unit had a narrow balcony for sun-drying laundry.

Danchi apartments were very popular through the 1960s because of their reasonable rent and reliable qualities. Each time when a new danchi was constructed, many more applications were filed than the number of available units, so tenants were chosen by lot. After around 1970, however, danchi apartments were built increasingly further away from downtown areas, and their rents were no longer attractive because of the steeply rising land prices all over the country.

Since the 1960s, private apartment units in various sizes, called *manshon* (mansions), have become popular among those who have given up the dream of owning a single-family house. These units are widespread in the 1990s. They are similar to condominiums in the United States. Occupants purchase the unit and partial rights to the land on which the building stands.

In large cities in Japan, renting an apartment is not easy. Because of the extreme housing shortage, landlords have a distinct advantage. Tenants are required to pay in advance nonrefundable fees equivalent to two or three months' rent in addition to the refundable deposit. Normally, an apartment unit does not come with refrigerator, kitchen stove, microwave oven, or washing machine.

Most people, even in large cities, consider apartments a temporary residence until they can afford to buy a house or condominium. For this reason, not much money is invested in apartment buildings. Thus, good-quality apartments are not easy to find at an affordable price for working people.

HISTORICAL ARCHITECTURE

Japanese architecture has been wooden architecture throughout its history. Shrines and temples were made of wood, and even castle buildings erected on the foundations of stonewalls had wooden frames. Throughout the centuries, the wooden architecture of Japan was honed into a refined system of structure and design.

Shinto Architecture

Shinto shrines are dedicated to deities (*kami*) and are often situated in beautiful mountains or deep forested areas venerated as sacred sites. Some shrines have no actual buildings but are simply marked as a sacred space by placing a sacred straw rope (*shimenawa*) around the site.

Shinto buildings date to the early agrarian period in Japan around 300 B.C. Single-story rectangular wooden buildings, they reflect the domestic architectural forms for dwellings or granaries. Their columns were raised high above the earth, and the veranda that encircled the building was reached by stairs. The roofs were thatched with natural materials, and crossbeams extended above the roof.

Although Shinto buildings were not built to last permanently, their forms have remained basically unchanged. Shrines are often rebuilt to purify the site and to renew the construction material, following the same designs as the previous ones. Buildings of the Ise shrine dedicated to Amaterasu, the Sun Goddess, and other legendary ancestors of the imperial family, have been rebuilt every twenty years faithfully following the traditional plans and technique. The carpenters (*miya-daiku*) who build and repair these shrines pass on their skills through the hereditary family lineage.

Some shrines from the Heian period onward were influenced by Chinese-style Buddhist architecture; they have elegantly curved roof lines, rainbow-shaped beams, and elaborate bracketing. Their pillars and beams were painted in brilliant vermilion. Additional buildings—such as prayer halls, treasure houses, accommodations for priests and worshippers, and open-air stages for performance of dance and music dedicated to the gods—are often connected by open-air corridors.

In terms of ornamentation, the Toshogu, the shrine dedicated to the founder of the Tokugawa *bakufu*, is the most famous and controversial. The shrine was completed in 1636 in the beautiful mountain setting of Nikko, northeast of Tokyo, and its buildings are elaborately embellished with carvings, sculpture, and other ornamentation. Visitors marvel at its craftsmanship, but critics have denounced it for being too gaudy and as the antithesis of the aesthetic qualities of Japanese art and architecture.

As the dwellings of deities, Shinto shrines protect trees and rocks within their compounds. Today in dense urban centers, shrines and temples remain as oases of greenery and open space.

Buddhist Architecture

When Buddhism was transmitted to Japan through China and Korea around the sixth century A.D., Buddhist arts and architecture also came along. The earliest temple buildings in Japan are reflections of the architecture of China and Korea at the time. A Buddhist temple was a place for worshipping Buddha. It was also a monastery where monks lived and studied Buddhist scriptures. A temple compound was laid out in a pattern known as *garan* (a term derived from the Sanskrit word meaning "communal dwelling"). The most essential buildings in the compound were the Pagoda, a multistoried tower where sacred relics believed to be a fraction of Buddha's remains were enshrined; the Main Hall called *kondo* (literally, golden hall) where the principal images of Buddha and other deities were housed; and the Lecture Hall where the monks received instructions and performed rituals. A corridor with a roof was built to connect the Main Hall and the Lecture Hall. A Drum Tower or Bell Tower was built to house a drum or bell that marked the time of daily observances in the monastery.

Storehouse buildings were the repositories of Buddhist scriptures and objects used for rituals. The monks lived in the dormitory in the compound. A kitchen building was built right next to the dormitory. The ground of the temple compound was enclosed by earthen walls which had openings at gates on each direction. Among the gates, the Great South Gate was the front or main gate of the temple.

Many of the hundreds of temples built in Nara and Kyoto survived after being repaired and rebuilt many times throughout the ages. Among them, Horyuji (seventh century) include the oldest wooden buildings.

After the twelfth century, Zen Buddhism was brought from China in the wake of renewed trade and diplomatic ties. As the Zen sect gained the patronage of samurai rulers, Zen-style architecture became fashionable. At a Zen temple, the meditation hall is very important. The largest among them, five major Zen monasteries were built in Kamakura; later another five were built in Kyoto under the patronage of the Kamakura and Ashikaga shogunates. Most of these are still well preserved and open to the public.

Castles

The history of construction of military fortification goes back to ancient times. However, castles as permanent fortifications and at the same time as administrative centers of territorial lords developed during the Warring States (1467–1568) and Azuchi-Momoyama (1568–1600) period. The castle architecture developed in this period became the standard architecture of the buildings of the headquarters of feudal lords throughout the Tokugawa period (1600–1868).

The entire castle structure rested on stone foundation walls that were surrounded with several rings of moats built for defensive purpose. The interior of the castle grounds was divided into several sections enclosed by stone walls, earth walls, or a moat. The central enclosure (*honmaru*) contained the donjon or the main tower complex (*tenshukaku*), the second enclosure (*ni no maru*) usually contained the lord's residence, and the third (*san no maru*) the residence of retainers. The most important building in the castle was the *tenshukaku*. The earliest tenshukaku was constructed at Azuchi castle of ODA Nobunaga. This castle, built on the shore of Lake Biwa of Shiga prefecture in the years 1576–1579, had a seven-storied tower that rose to a height of 32.5 meters (105 feet) above the top of the stone foundation walls and 46 meters (151 feet) including the foundation walls. Loopholes were made on the walls to observe the outside and for shooting bullets.

Azuchi castle was destroyed soon after the death of Oda Nobunaga. Later, even larger and more sumptuous castles were built at Osaka (1583), Fushimi (1594), Himeji (1609), Nagoya (1612), and Edo (1636). Edo castle, the headquarters of Tokugawa shogunate, is located in the center of Tokyo and has been used as the imperial palace since 1869.

MODERN ARCHITECTURE AND ARCHITECTS

The earliest examples of modern Western-style architecture in Japan were houses built by the Europeans who came to Nagasaki, Yokohama, and other port cities in the mid-nineteenth century. These houses were colonial-style with verandas, reflecting the homes of Europeans who lived in colonies in India and Southeast Asia. The house of Thomas B. Glover, an English trader, in Nagasaki is a famous example.

The Meiji government hired European engineers to build Western-style buildings for newly created government offices, schools, banks, factories, railway stations, and other institutions. In Hokkaido, the first Western-style buildings were built by Americans who came to introduce American-style agriculture.

The government also invited European architects to train Japanese architects. The first instructor was an Englishman, Josiah Conder (1852–1920), who taught at the Industrial College (later, the School of Engineering at the University of Tokyo). He arrived in Tokyo in 1877 and stayed in Japan for the rest of his life, honored as the teacher of the first generation modern architects of Japan. To this day, a bronze statue of Conder stands before the building of the Department of Architecture of the University of Tokyo, the most prestigious and influential institution where architects are trained in Japan today.

Conder himself designed and supervised the construction of Western-style buildings, including Rokumeikan (completed in 1883), the state reception hall for entertaining foreign dignitaries, and Mitsubishi no. one building (1894), Japan's first multiple-story office building of red brick. Among the monumental buildings designed by the students of Conder are the main office building of the Bank of Japan (completed in 1896), the Akasaka Detached Palace (1909), and Tokyo Station buildings (1914). These reflect nineteenth-century European-style structure; however, the architects subtly incorporated traditional Japanese motifs in the decoration. After the turn of the twentieth century, American-style high-rise office buildings began to appear in the business districts of Tokyo and Yokohama and, after World War I, became the model for office building architecture.

Frank Lloyd Wright (1867–1959) and Antonin Raymond (1888–1976) of the United States and Bruno Taut (1880–1938) of Germany, who came to Japan after World War I, were greatly interested in the Japanese architectural tradition, and their works influenced Western architecture. They also encouraged Japanese architects to re-evaluate traditional Japanese architecture. Subsequent renewed interest in traditional design led to the development of a new residential style that assimilated traditional elements, such as *sukiya-zukuri*, which originated as a small building for the tea ceremony.

Throughout the history of modern architecture in Japan, a constant dilemma facing architects was how and how much to reconcile traditional forms with modern science and technology. This issue became even more important in the postwar years. When the Architectural Institute of Japan Award (the most prestigious prize of this kind in Japan) was established in 1949, the first one was given to TANIGUCHI Yoshiro. He designed a monument to the writer Shimazaki Toson in Nagano prefecture, and his innovative use of traditional architectural forms won him the award. The works of other award-winning architects in more recent years reveal an increasing interest in the bold use of traditional forms. Creative designs blending traditional elements and technology have been internationally recognized.

As an educator at the most influential school of architecture in Japan and as a prominent architect, MAEKAWA Kunio (1905–1986) was a leading figure in Japanese architecture from the late 1930s through the postwar era. After graduating from the University of Tokyo in 1928, he went to Paris to study under Le Corbusier (1887–1965) for two years. After returning to Japan, he worked with Antonin Raymond (1888–1976), who stayed in Japan from 1919 to 1937, and started an architectural firm in 1935. Maekawa greatly influenced the world of architecture in postwar Japan, not only in designing office buildings, public halls, and apartment buildings but also as professor of architecture at the University of Tokyo. Another leading architect of the time, SAKAKURA Junzo (1904–1968), also worked with Le Corbusier in Paris during the early 1930s. The international style of modernist architecture brought back by Maekawa and Sakakura generated great enthusiasm in Japan. The younger generation who followed them produced internationally acclaimed works in the postwar world.

During the 1960s, when dynamic economic growth promoted a construction boom in Japan, large construction companies specializing in standardized, characterless structures thrived. In Japanese cities, box-like gray concrete buildings became ubiquitous. Commercialization of architecture and construction was an inevitable part of postwar economic development. In the early 1970s the first skyscrapers appeared in the Shinjuku area, a commercial, transportation, and entertainment center of downtown Tokyo. Shinjuku had been designated as a special subcenter of the Tokyo metropolis to supplement the old center near the government headquarters.

During another economic boom of the 1980s, large-scale construction projects of monumental buildings, as symbols of commercial wealth and political authority, were initiated. Some were completed in the early 1990s. A prominent example is the New Tokyo Metropolitan Government Head-quarters in Shinjuku, which was completed in 1991. It is the largest set of buildings constructed in twentieth-century Japan. It is comprised of a series of skyscrapers centered around twin towers 243 meters high, interlinked buildings, and a civic plaza.

The New Tokyo Metropolitan Government Headquarters was designed by TANGE Kenzo (1913–   ), a leading figure among contemporary archi-tects in Japan and an internationally acclaimed city planner. Tange studied under the Maekawa Kunio at the University of Tokyo, began his activities during the war, taught at the University of Tokyo, and trained many out-standing architects. He had passionately admired the style of Le Corbusier ever since he was a student, and he pledged to follow that tradition. He moved ahead of Maekawa and Sakakura to design monumental buildings with impressive dynamism. Moreover, his ambition expanded to include designing larger environments as an urban planner. He participated in the city planning for Tokyo in 1960 and later in planning for the new capital in Nigeria. Among his early monumental works are the Hiroshima Peace Center (1956), the first Tokyo Metropolitan Government Headquarters located at Yurakucho (1959), and the Yoyogi Gymnasium complex for the Tokyo Olympics of 1964.

To find out about the most famous architectural projects of recent years, it is useful to see the beautifully produced photographs in bilingual period-icals such as *Japan Architect* (published by Shinkenchikusha) as well as other Japanese-language periodicals on architecture. They report not only on large-scale public projects such as Kansai International Airport terminal building, city halls, art museums, and public libraries, but also single-family houses and smaller-scale public buildings such as retirement homes for disabled citizens. It is noteworthy that many buildings designed by prominent archi-tects during the 1980s and 1990s were built for prefectural and municipal government-sponsored projects in various locations in Japan. Excellent architectural works are no longer limited to state-sponsored buildings in To-kyo, Osaka, or Kyoto.

It is noteworthy that most of the accomplished Japanese architects started as students of architecture at major universities, especially the University of Tokyo, where they studied under masters like Maekawa Kunio and Tange Kenzo. Other universities with distinguished architecture departments include Tokyo Geijutsu Daigaku (Tokyo University of Fine Arts and Music), Waseda University, and Nippon Daigaku. Many of the most influential architects maintain their ties with universities and often teach there as faculty members.

Among the most active architects, however, the training of ANDO Tadao (1941–) is exceptional. He is essentially a self-taught architect without an authoritative academic background. He designed many residences with special attention to the harmonious relationship between building and natural surroundings. He successfully blends the aesthetic elements of traditional houses with functionally modern structures.

GARDENS

Japanese gardens incorporate natural slopes, rocks, sand, water, trees, and plants. A garden is meant to be a replica of the scenic beauty of nature or an imagined paradise, or an expression of an entire universe in a limited space. The Japanese love of natural beauty and their sensitivity to the changes of seasons are reflected in their gardens.

The ancient origin of landscaping and garden building was in the demarcation of sacred spaces with hedges. This was based on the belief that gods dwelt in unusual rock formations, dense clusters of trees, or waterfalls. Naturally formed boulders are still highly valued in gardens in Japan today. When Buddhism was introduced from China and Korea, Chinese-style Buddhist architecture accompanied it, and stone foundations, bridges, and other Chinese architectural elements enriched the Japanese view of architecture and garden design.

Heian period aristocrats built gardens as an integral part of their mansions, a style known as *shinden-zukuri* (main hall–style mansion). In this design the main hall was open to the garden on the south. It was used for official receptions and other formal occasions. Accompanying buildings behind (on the north) and on the east and west sides of the main hall were family living quarters. The buildings were covered with thatched roofs and had elevated floors and steps connecting the floor with the ground at the entrance. All the buildings were connected with covered corridors. The corridors attached to the buildings on the east and west wings were extended toward the south into the garden. At the end of these corridors, pavilions for fishing were built over a pond. Earthen walls were built around the entire mansion compound. In the space between the earthen walls and extended corridors were located shelters for ox-drawn carts and housing for servants and guardsmen. In the center of the garden was a pond large enough for boating, and its water streamed between the buildings to convey a sense of coolness in summer. In the middle of the pond was an islet. The most famous garden of the Heian period is that of Byodoin temple in Uji, a suburb of Kyoto. It was modeled after the image of paradise (*jodo*) described in the scriptures of the Jodo sect of Buddhism. Such gardens centered on a large pond are classified as *funa-asobi* (pleasure boat) style.

The warriors who became the ruling elite during the Kamakura period patronized temples and monasteries of Zen Buddhism. Zen monks who had skills in constructing gardens created a new style of landscape gardens known as *kare-sansui* (literally, "dry mountain stream" or "waterless rock and sand garden"). The rock garden of Ryoanji temple in Kyoto built during the Muromachi period is a well-known example. It is composed of rocks laid out on white sand in an enclosed rectangular space between the temple building and the earthen walls surrounding the temple compound. The rocks and white sand symbolize land and ocean, or the whole universe, in the same spirit as landscape painting, *bonsai* (potted dwarf trees), and tray landscaping do. This type of garden is meticulously composed to be viewed from within the building as a form of contemplation. They are classified as *kansho* (contemplation) style.

Those who built tea ceremony rooms paid careful attention to gardens. To provide serenity inside the tea room, a garden served as a protective buffer from the world of hustle and bustle. Guests of the tea ceremony were guided to the room along a narrow path through groves of trees in the garden, walking over stepping stones and stopping at a stone basin to rinse their hands and mouth before entering the room. Stone lanterns were essential fixtures of this type of garden. Most gardens of residential architecture built before World War II were constructed in the same spirit and form as the landscape gardens of tea ceremony rooms. This was a natural result of standard houses of the time being modeled after *shoin-zukuri* (studio style) buildings that developed during the Muromachi period.

Gardens of large mansions or richly endowed Buddhist temples were designed to take the viewers through various scenes. Classified as *shuyu* (stroll) gardens, these include gardens attached to the tea ceremony rooms of the Zen temples Jishoji (known as Ginkakuji, or the Temple of the Silver Pavilion) and Rokuonji (known as Kinkakuji, or the Temple of the Golden Pavilion).

Many public gardens in Japan today used to be the private gardens of feudal lords. Syntheses of various elements of preceding forms, they are identified as *kaiyu* (many-pleasure) style because they present strikingly different scenes as one walks through them. Typically they are constructed around a central pond, narrow streams, landscaped hills, groves of trees, arbors with thatched roofs, and flower gardens. Among the largest and most famous gardens of this type are Ritsurin Park in the city of Takamatsu in Shikoku, roughly 750,000 square meters in area; the garden of Hama Detached Palace in Tokyo; Kenroku-en park in Kanazawa city; Koraku-en (*en* means "garden") in Okayama city and in Tokyo; and the garden of the Katsura Detached Palace in Kyoto, which was built as a resort house of the imperial household. All were constructed during the Tokugawa period.

NOTE

1. *Asahi shimbun Japan Almanac* (Tokyo: Asahi Shimbunsa, 1997), p. 204; Nihon Tokei Kyokai, comp., *Tokei de miru Nihon, 1996* (Tokyo: Nihon Tokei Kyokai, 1996), p. 78.

6

Cuisine

Typical Japanese Meals Today

Meals in Japan range from traditional cuisine to more convenient Western-style fare. It is often said that younger people are weaning themselves from the rice-centered traditional meal. Also, increasing numbers of people regularly eat fast food or ready-to-eat food sold in the basement food sections of department stores or at neighborhood convenience stores.

What do average Japanese people eat every day? Before answering this question, we must point out that the majority of Japanese today are urban residents.[1] Workers of all kinds—including professionals, office workers, and blue-collar workers—commute to the work place. Because their salary is determined on a monthly basis and they are paid once a month, in Japan they are called salary men, almost a synonym for average urban worker. What do they and their families eat?

One way to get a general idea about what ordinary Japanese eat is to look into stores where most people do everyday grocery shopping. Many people, including housewives and business people, shop for food almost every day. Even though almost all households have refrigerators, people still prefer to get fresh food. There used to be a green grocer, fish market, butcher, liquor store, and general food store in every neighborhood, and housewives shopped there as a daily routine. These "mom and pop" stores were run by people who lived in the same building as the shops. Since the economic growth of the 1960s, most of these neighborhood stores have disappeared. In their place, every neighborhood nowadays has one or more supermarkets.

Supermarkets in Japanese neighborhoods are much smaller than their counterparts in the United States. Shoppers in Japan mostly come on foot or by bicycle. Even for those who have a family car, it is more convenient to walk or ride on a bike because parking spaces are very limited and traffic is heavy. Moreover, many neighborhood supermarkets are too small for using shopping carts, and shoppers have to carry goods in baskets. It means that people can buy only as much as they can carry without a cart or car. Therefore food items are packaged in small quantities. For example, the standard size of a milk carton is one-quarter gallon. Moreover, standard refrigerators in Japan are much smaller than those in American households, because Japanese houses are small and electricity is expensive. More important, however, people strongly prefer to buy fresh fish and vegetables every single day.

Fish, an important source of protein, is the main dish in traditional Japanese cuisine. In a supermarket in Japan, the fish section is normally bigger than the meat section. Unlike a traditional fish market where the shopkeeper cleans the fish for each customer who buys it, fish at supermarkets are already cleaned, cut into serving portions, or even sliced as *sashimi*. Aside from fresh fish, marinated, salted, pickled, and dried kinds are sold. *Katsuobushi* (dried bonito filet), the most important ingredient for soup stock in Japanese cooking, is sold as flakes or powder and packed in convenient small packages.

Most shoppers at neighborhood stores are housewives, but it is not at all unusual to see men there as well. It was considered unbecoming for a man to shop at grocery stores thirty years ago, but no longer. Young men do not seem to have any inhibition about shopping for food or cooking at home, which used to be regarded as the exclusive domain of women. The main reason why most shoppers are women is that men who commute to work are rarely back from work before dinnertime. If both the man and woman in a family work, it is still the woman's job to shop and cook dinner after work.

Breakfast

Most Japanese urbanites today have a Western-style breakfast. Typically it consists of fruit, eggs, and toast, which they have with milk, black tea, or coffee. It takes much less time to prepare this kind of breakfast than to cook a traditional Japanese breakfast. For those who do not have time for even a simple breakfast at home, nutrition drinks with vitamin additives are sold at newspaper stands in train stations.

Traditional breakfast requires cooking rice, making *miso* soup, grilling dried fish, and slicing pickled vegetables. During summer and autumn, *nukazuke*, or pickled cucumbers, eggplants, or turnips made in seasoned and fermented rice bran, is highly desired. Fermented soy beans, called *natto*, is a familiar breakfast food eaten with steaming hot rice. Very often *natto* is served with raw egg. Also popular is raw egg flavored with soy sauce poured over a bowl of steaming hot rice. For a typical family, the norm used to be that everyone ate together at the dining table. Nowadays this custom is disappearing, and Western-style breakfast is easily prepared individually.

For travelers desiring a traditional Japanese breakfast, the best place to stay would be a traditional Japanese inn, which normally includes breakfast as part of the room charges. In the past, breakfasts served at inns were delivered to guests' rooms, but now they are more often served in the dining hall. Also, guests are given a choice between Western and Japanese-style breakfasts because more people prefer the Western style.

Lunch

A box lunch, called *bento*, is the most common for eating away from home. A very elaborate box lunch called *makunouchi bento* comes with a full-course menu including fish, meat, vegetable, sweets, and always rice, which occupies at least half the box. Some lunches come in two boxes to serve rice and other food separately. Box lunches are sold at traditional theaters where performances used to last a whole day, railway stations, airport restaurants, and convenience stores that sell ready-to-eat meals. Before the age of high-speed trains, box lunches with local produce were sold at local stations. Vendors on the platform walked up to the train and sold the lunch and tea through the windows.

For traditional housewives, it was (and still is regarded to be) a labor of love to make box lunches for outings and for those who eat lunch at work or at school. It takes more work to make a box lunch than to prepare a meal to eat at home. Food for box lunches cannot be perishable or juicy. A variety of foods in small amounts must be arranged attractively. Of course, there are simpler box lunches. The simplest one, called *hinomaru bento* (rising sun box lunch), has only a plum pickled with red herb in the middle of white rice packed in a rectangular lunch box. An even simpler method is to make a rice ball instead of using a lunch box. As a result of the proliferation of fast food and ready-to-eat meals, fewer people take homemade lunches nowadays. Workers in urban centers are more likely to eat at restaurants or get takeout.

Dinner

Nowadays, people eat a great variety of food for the main meal, and it is more difficult to define a "typical" Japanese dinner than to talk about a typical breakfast or lunch. Nevertheless, the traditional concept of a complete meal—that is, a meal made up of staple food (*shushoku*) and accompanying dishes (*okazu*)—is still shared by the Japanese today.

The standard staple food has been rice (short-grain Japonica variety). Other grains or potatoes are substitutes. Cooked rice (*gohan* or *meshi*) is the main part of a meal; in fact, the word *gohan* or *meshi* also means "meal." Breakfast is *asa-gohan* or *asa-meshi* (morning meal), lunch is *hiru-gohan* or *hiru-meshi* (noon meal), and supper is *ban-gohan* or *ban-meshi* (evening meal). Rice is cooked without seasoning and served in a small ceramic bowl along with a bowl of soup and other dishes. Chopsticks made of wood, bamboo, or plastic are used to eat from the rice bowl or soup bowl. The proper manner is to hold the bowl with one hand and use the chopsticks with the other. Since rice is so important in Japanese meals, people are sensitive to subtle differences in its texture and flavor, and various strains have been developed in different parts of the country. Popular varieties are Koshihikari and Sasanishiki. Among the younger generation, however, rice consumption has been decreasing in recent years, whereas consumption of meat and dairy products has increased.

As to *okazu* (accompanying dishes), the most common items are various kinds of seafood from nearby coasts and distant oceans, beef, pork, chicken, eggs, soybean products such as bean curd, and vegetables of the season. The season's earliest shipment of vegetables or fish is called *hatsumono* and is valued as the harbinger of the season. For example, bonito (a type of tuna) start to show up in May when the trees leaf out. The height of the season, called *shun*, occurs when the best quality is attained. Although seafood has been an important source of protein ever since prehistoric Japan, the history of beef in Japan is relatively new. The famous Japanese dish *sukiyaki* was created in the nineteenth century when Europeans introduced beef.

Most home cooking nowadays is done on a gas range, which has long replaced stoves that burned charcoal, firewood, or straw. For cooking rice, almost every family uses an electric rice-cooker. Although ovens for baking and broiling are not standard household appliances, microwave ovens have become quite popular.

For seasoning of food, soy sauce (*shoyu*) and fermented bean paste (*miso*), as well as salt and sugar, are most commonly used. *Sake*, pepper, Japanese horseradish (*wasabi*), and sesame oil are flavorings. Stock for soup and for cooking vegetables is made from dried bonito flakes (*katsuobushi*), dried kelp, and dried baby sardines (*niboshi*). For frying, most people use vegetable oil such as mustard seed oil.

In Japanese cuisine, the highest value is placed on freshness and enhancement of the innate flavor and texture of the ingredients. Therefore, quick and simple cooking with minimal seasoning is preferred. *Sashimi* (sliced fillet of raw fish or raw shellfish) is one of the most popular items in the Japanese menu.

To know about traditional Japanese meals in daily life, it is useful to know how formal banquet meals are prepared and served. The kinds of food, the cooking methods, and the manner of serving and eating meals at home and at restaurants today are consistent with the principles of traditional formal banquets. The manners and customs of serving and eating formal banquet meals filtered down to commoners' households and became the model. At home or at other places, everyone is supposed to say "*itadaki-masu*" ("I gratefully have this meal") before starting to eat, and at the end, "*gochisosama deshita*" ("thank you for the feast"), even if it was a very simple meal.

TRADITIONAL BANQUET FOOD

There are three types of traditional banquet food: *honzenryori* (the most formal banquet food), *chakaiseki ryori* (the meal served at a tea ceremony), and *kaiseki ryori* (general banquet food). For all types of banquets, one serving portion of each food is served in a separate plate or bowl, all of which are arranged on a lacquered wooden tray for each guest. The tray is placed on the tatami floor before each guest. The size of the tray is about one square foot, and some trays have legs. Aside from the primary tray, a second and third tray may be served at a banquet with many courses.

Honzen Ryori

Honzen ryori is a development from ritual banquets for court nobles during the Heian period. Its roots go back to the traditions of Tang Dynasty China. The basic menu of honzen ryori consists of rice, one kind of soup, and three kinds of accompanying dishes, which are typically *sashimi*, grilled fish, and stewed vegetable. Other combinations are two kinds of soup and five kinds of dishes, or three kinds of soup and seven kinds of dishes. Rice and pickled vegetables are always served but not counted in the number of items served.

The dishes are placed on a tray in a prescribed arrangement. Bowls and plates are carefully chosen to match the ingredients and the season of the year. The artistic appeal of the dish is important because a dish must be visually delightful in order to taste good. There are strict rules concerning the order of eating the food and drinking the *sake* during the meal. The guest must first eat a small bite of rice and then have a sip of soup. Thereafter, he or she must eat another bite of rice, then eat from one of the dishes, and finish the soup. One must not go directly from one dish to another without taking a bite of rice. The pickles are not to be touched until the very end of the meal, when they are eaten with the remaining rice.

Chakaiseki Ryori

Chakaiseki ryori literally means "tea" and "[warm] stone in the robe." It developed from the meals at Zen monasteries together with the tea ceremony. It is supposed to be a frugal meal, as its name came from the fact that Zen monks in training placed warm stones inside their robes to stave off hunger. The food is served at tea ceremony now. The basic menu consists of one soup (typically *miso* soup) and three dishes of seasonal fish or vegetable served with rice. In addition, a light soup called *hashi arai* (rinsing chopsticks) and assorted appetizers called *hassun* (literally, "eight-inch [tray]") can be added. Small side dishes called *mukozuke*—which could be *sashimi*, marinated fish, or fresh vegetable—are also served.

Kaiseki Ryori

Kaiseki ryori literally means "the meal for dinner party." It is less formal than the above two types. Today, traditional Japanese-style party meals are served at *ryotei* (Japanese-style restaurants of the highest class), wedding banquets, and other social gatherings. The general principle is to serve various kinds of appetizers, clear soup, and dishes of grilled, steamed, stewed, and deep-fried food, including fish, meat, and vegetables. Warm *sake* is always served in small ceramic bottles; a tiny cup containing just enough *sake* for one big sip is provided for each guest. Rice with pickled vegetables is served at the very end of the meal.

Sweets

It is noteworthy that there was no concept of dessert in traditional Japanese cuisine. Instead, sweet dishes are served as a part of the meal. At the tea ceremony, sweets are served before the tea. It is also customary in entertaining dinner guests at home to serve tea with sweets before the dinner. The most common ingredients of sweets are beans, agar-agar (a kind of sea plant), and rice powder. Oil or eggs are rarely used in traditional sweets. Nowadays, of course, all sorts of sweets of foreign origins are very popular. Some of the most popular are combinations of Japanese and Western ideas. For example, *an-pan* is a bun with sweet bean paste inside.

RESTAURANTS

To have a family dinner or dinner with friends at a restaurant was not customary in Japan until very recently, when people started to own cars. Now new types of restaurants for family outings have appeared. Dinners at restaurants are primarily for social entertainment. The variety of restaurants in Tokyo is just as great as in New York City. Japanese restaurants include *ryotei*, high-class places where the most exquisite meals are served in Japanese-style private dining rooms by highly refined hostesses wearing Japanese outfits; and small restaurants where only *domburi* (rice covered with some sort of cooked meat with egg and vegetable, served in a large ball), noodles, curry rice (Japanese-style Indian food), or other one-course meals are served.

Many restaurants specialize in French, Italian, Chinese, and other famous cuisine. They claim to live up to the world's highest standards, although most dishes of foreign origin are subtly modified to suit the Japanese taste. Because of the absence of strong ethnic communities in Japan, almost all customers are Japanese. Average salary men would not dine at the highest-rated restaurants except when entertaining for business. For lunch, however, they usually leave their offices to eat at restaurants.

Lunchtime in Japan is rather short, and restaurants are open for lunch only between 11:00 and 2:00. Since just about everyone rushes to restaurants during these hours, popular places are very crowded and therefore no one can eat in a leisurely fashion. For talking with friends or passing time by oneself, there are coffee shops nearby. Although many restaurants serve a variety of food, small restaurants specializing in traditional lunch fare such as *soba* (buckwheat noodles served in various styles), *sushi* (rice seasoned with vinegar, often served with sliced raw fish), or *unagi* (eel broiled in soy sauce-based sauce, always served with rice) are ever popular. If you miss lunch during these hours, it may be difficult to find a place to eat unless you are located near a McDonald's or a department store. Most department stores have one or two floors for restaurants that offer various kinds of food at any time while the stores are open. Department store restaurants and any other restaurants that cater to the public display plastic models of food items with price tags so that customers can tell exactly what kind of food is served.

Many small restaurants in downtown areas open again in the early evening to serve drinks and small dishes for salary men who stop by with their colleagues after work. Some of them go home for dinner, but occasionally they move on to a series of bars to spend all night drinking. This is quite normal. When they arrive home, they are either too drunk to eat or not hungry enough to have a full dinner. They just eat *ochazuke* (a bowl of rice on which hot green tea is poured, normally served with dried seafood or pickles). Many of those who come home late at night have not necessarily been drinking. Middle managers and career bureaucrats often work late in their offices, especially during busy seasons. Those who do not have time to go out to eat get food delivered, such as *sushi, soba,* and *domburi.* Other varieties of food, including American pizza, can also be ordered for delivery.

NOTE

1. According to the 1995 census, 78.1 percent of the population are residents of cities. See Nihon Tokei Kyokai, comp., *Tokei de miru Nihon, 1996* (Tokyo: Nihon Tokei Kyokai, 1996), p. 34.

During the 1960s through the 1980s, the trend for population to be concentrated in large cities caused depopulation of the rural areas. As of 1995, 43 percent of the Japanese live in the three largest metropolitan areas, namely, Tokyo, Osaka, and Nagoya metropolitan areas. See *Asahi Shimbun Japan Almanac* (Tokyo: Asahi Shimbunsha, 1997), p. 52.

Many people who live in townships and villages in rural areas commute to neighboring cities as "salary men." Those who work in the primary industries (agriculture, fishing, forestry, and mining) represent 5.7 percent of the entire population. Among many farmers' households some members of the family—normally men—commute to cities to work, leaving farm work to their retired parents and wives.

7

Clothing

Everyday Japanese clothing is just the same as in industrialized countries. From work clothes to sleepwear, the modern world appears to share a common style and material for clothing. The following discussion is mainly about traditional Japanese clothing, which is no longer a part of everyday life and is reserved for special ceremonial occasions.

The Japanese adopted Western-style clothing in the mid-nineteenth century as part of the modernization program. In the very beginning, the government adopted Western-style uniforms for military men and policemen, and it required civilian officials to wear Western suits at work. The imperial family adopted European-style costume for public ceremonies, especially those for foreign guests. For schoolboys and students in high schools and universities, military-style uniforms were adopted. Uniforms for primary and high school students are still common in Japan today. Up to the 1960s many college students were required to wear college uniforms, and it was important for them to appear in uniform at job interviews. Today college uniforms have totally disappeared.

For everyday life in prewar Japan, traditional Japanese-style clothing was much more economical and practical. Western-style clothes (*yofuku*) were expensive to buy and to clean, and most people felt they were rather uncomfortable. A common practice among those who worked in government or business offices was to change to Japanese-style everyday outfits upon returning home. Artisans and farmers had traditional clothes that suited their work. Artisans and store hands displayed their store logo on the back of their cotton jackets (*happi*) or on their aprons. Even though Western-style work clothes became common by the time of World War II, people who worked in traditional trades maintained their traditional work clothes. Their clothing, footwear, and other items indicated their line of trade. Nowadays everyone wears Western-style dress such as T-shirt and blue jeans, and it is impossible to tell the occupation of men on the street.

For most Japanese today, Western-style clothes are for everyday wear, and Japanese-style clothes (*wafuku*) are only for ceremonial occasions. The term *wafuku* was created to distinguish Japanese-style clothes from Western-style (*yofuku*). It is used as a synonym for *kimono*, which literally means "clothing" but is used to refer to Japanese-style clothes. Today people in kimono are rarely seen on the streets, except during the New Years season or on other holidays when many people (especially women) wear kimono. (In addition to performers of traditional art, hostesses of high-class Japanese restaurants work in kimono.) This does not mean, however, that Japanese people do not like the kimono. On the contrary, they believe it is the most aesthetically pleasing clothing and that they look the best in it. The kimono section of department stores often takes up an entire floor.

Just as in any society, there are rules in Japan about the types and color of clothing people wear on various occasions. The rules about kimono are more important in Japan than rules about Western clothes. Kimono reflects a time past when social codes concerning status were important. Also, the distinction between formal and informal situations was taken seriously.

For all kinds of kimono, the cut and tailoring are basically the same for men and women. Types are distinguished by fabric, method of weaving, and color and designs of the fabric. Kimono fabric comes in rolls about 12 yards long and 14 inches wide. This is enough to make one adult's kimono of all sizes and styles. To make a kimono, the fabric is cut in eight pieces: the two main sections (*migoro*), the two front sections (*okumi*), two sleeves (*sode*), and collar (*eri*) and over-collar (*tome-eri*). The sleeves vary in length according to the type of kimono.

Kimono may be lined (*awase*), unlined (*hitoe*), or cotton/silk-floss quilted (*wataire*). An unlined kimono is worn only from June through September if it is used as formal dress. The Japanese are very sensitive about proper clothing reflecting the change of seasons. Even after switching to Western-style clothes, they maintained this sensitivity. The first days of June and October are the days for changing clothes. Those who get uniforms for summer and for the rest of the seasons must change on these days. The uniforms of workers at train stations, bus drivers, and high-school girls are most visible, and all of them change to white summer uniform starting on June 1. *Yukata* (stencil-dyed cotton kimono) is the most common summer outfit for everyday use. Cotton/silk-floss quilted kimono for winter is worn only at home.

MEN'S KIMONO

Today, very few men wear kimono in public except for those who perform some sort of traditional art. Men's formal kimono is lustrous *habutae* silk in black. The only decoration is the family crest (*mon*) in white, which is either stencil-dyed or embroidered. The family crest appears in five spots on a formal kimono (*montsuki*): back center, front panels on each side, and on the back of each sleeve. For semi-formal kimono, the family crest appears in three spots: on the back center and on each of the sleeves. The same *montsuki* for men can be worn for festive occasions or for mourning. For very formal occasions, men must don on top of the montsuki a *haori* (half-length over-kimono) and *hakama* (wide trousers or skirt made of silk). For semi-formal occasions, the kimono can be another dark color. For less formal wear, kimono and haori may be made of wool, cotton, linen, or synthetic fabrics.

WOMEN'S KIMONO

There are more different kinds of kimono for women than for men, and more women wear kimono than men do. The generation of women who grew up before the war sewed kimono for the entire family. To clean good-quality kimono, they would take apart all sections and sew the pieces together again after washing. Caring for kimono took a lot of work, but women after marriage wore their good-quality kimono for their lifetime and even handed them down to their daughters.

There are different kinds of formal kimono for women for festive occasions and for mourning. Also, a woman must choose the right color and design according to her age and marital status.

For unmarried young women, the most formal kimono for festive occasions is *furisode* in various colors. It has an overall design that runs diagonally from the shoulder down to the hem. It is characterized by long sleeves. Sleeves of the *oofurisode* (big *furisode*) are long enough to reach the hem, and sleeves of the *chufurisode* (medium *furisode*) are a little shorter. The *oofurisode* is worn by brides during their wedding banquet; therefore wedding guests are supposed to refrain from wearing it in deference to the bride.

For married women, the most formal kimono for festive occasions is the *tomesode* of black silk crepe (*chirimen*) with the family crest in five spots. It is also called edozuma. It has a design only on the hem. To wear it properly, the *maru-obi* or *obi* (sash)of double thickness, or *fukuro-obi* (lined *obi*) made of gold and silver brocade often in bird-and-flower designs, or its equivalent, is required. At a wedding reception, black *tomesode* is a must for a woman who serves as a *nakoodo* (go-between) and the most appropriate clothing for relatives of the bride and groom.

The tomesode in plain color other than black is called *iro-tomesode*. If it has the family crest in five spots, it is regarded as formal wear like the black tomesode. The color must be chosen to match the age of the wearer. As a general rule, the older the woman is, the more somber the color she is supposed to wear. If the family crest is placed in three spots only, it becomes less formal. The *iro-tomesode* with family crest in three spots is regarded as just right for a wedding guest who is not related to the marrying couple.

For less formal festive occasions, married and unmarried women of all ages can wear *homongi*, which is made of the same kind of silk as the furisode or tomesode and comes in various colors with designs from the shoulder to the hem. It is possible to make a *homongi* a semi-formal kimono by putting the family crest in three spots or one in the center back. Silk kimono with small overall print (*komon*) is for less formal social occasions and for town wear.

For funerals, married and unmarried women of all ages can wear a *montsuki* of plain black silk over a white silk under-kimono (*nagajuban*) and black *obi* and black accessories.

With the kimono, various kinds of long sashes (*obi*) are worn. Men wear *kaku-obi*, 3-inch-wide stiff silk tied in a half-bow, or *heko-obi*, a soft black or gray silk obi that is at least 20 inches wide and long enough to wrap around the body two or three times; it is worn tied or tucked in just under the waist. Women's obi is made of silk about one foot wide and 10 to 13 feet long. It is tied in the back in various fashions depending on the age and marital status of the wearer. The most common way to tie obi for an adult woman is with *otaiko*, a square-shaped bow. The *hitoe* (unlined) *obi* is for summer season. *Maru-obi* (obi of double width) and *fukuro-obi* (lined obi) are for formal kimono. *Nagoya-obi* (folded obi) is for both formal and informal occasions. Obi for formal wear requires special quality silk and costs several times the price of kimono. There are obi for daily wear and cotton summer kimono.

To wear a formal kimono, especially for women, a whole set of accessories is necessary. As no buttons or fasteners are used, kimono and under-kimono are held in place by many cloth cords and belts. The footwear for kimono is *zori* (platform sandals) or *geta* (wooden stilted sandals with thongs). The following are the most basic necessities required to get dressed in kimono: a pair of *tabi* (white socks with slit between big toe and the other toes), *juban* (undershirt for kimono), *koshimaki* (wrap-around underskirt), *nagajuban* (full-size under-kimono made of white or plain silk), white *han'eri* (collar to be stitched on *nagajuban), datemaki* (a wide belt to wrap around the waist over the *nagajuban), obi* (sash), *obiita* (stiff panel to insert under the obi in front to keep it from wrinkling), *obimakura* (small cushion to fill out the square bow of obi on the back), *obiage* (a sash to hold the cushion in place), and *obijime* (a narrow band tied around the obi to keep the bow in the right shape).

The kimono is fitted on the body with all the seams straight, and the length is adjusted by tucking in the excess material under the sash. One absolutely important rule is to pull tight the right side of the front first and then the left side over it. The opposite is done only for dressing the dead when they are being readied for the coffin.

It takes training and experience to put on kimono comfortably and attractively. It also requires training in walking and moving gracefully when wearing kimono. Since most Japanese people do not wear it in daily life anymore, professional help is available for putting on formal kimono at beauty shops or schools for dressing up in kimono. For less formal kimono, various convenient devices, such as *tsuke-obi* (sash with ready-made bow) and *hiyoku shitate* (white collar fixed under the kimono), are widely used. Indeed, wearing kimono is one of the traditional arts that is no longer a part of everyday life for most Japanese people.

8

Women, Marriage, and Family

The position of women in the Japanese family and society has changed a great deal since World War II. Under the New Constitution that stipulated equality between the sexes, Japanese women gained voting rights, the right to inherit family property in the equal shares with their male siblings, and the right to receive the same education as men.

The number of working women has increased steadily. The number of married women who work after age 35 increased from 32.7 percent of female work force in 1962 to 57.2 percent in 1995. In the past, female employees were generally young unmarried women who worked until marriage or the birth of their first child. The traditional thinking that men should work and women should keep house is still strong among men. However, according to a survey by the prime minister's office, the percentage of women who agree with this thinking sharply declined from 35.7 in 1979 to 22.3 in 1995.

In theory, women are guaranteed equal opportunity and treatment in all phases of employment by the Equal Employment Opportunity Law of 1985. Nevertheless, Japanese women have a long way to go to obtain equal opportunities in the job market. About 33 percent of women employees work "part-time," which means that they work fewer than 35 hours per week and are paid much less than full-time workers. Women account for about 67 percent of part-time workers. In comparison to the United States, there are far fewer women in Japan in public office, senior-level corporate management, or any position of power and prestige. According to 1994 government statistics, only 8.7 percent of managerial jobs were held by women. Women made up 6.9 percent of the country's lawyers and 5.1 percent of certified accountants. To achieve full equality in real life, Japanese women face obstacles similar to those American women have experienced.[1]

TRADITIONAL MARRIAGE AND THE FAMILY SYSTEM

In order to focus on problems that characterize the situation of women in Japan, we must discuss the traditional Japanese family system and its underlying concepts. In many ways these concepts are still upheld, which makes family members responsible for helping individuals in the family who need assistance. In prewar Japan, the basic framework that defined the place of men and women was the family system, known as the *ie* system. *Ie* refers to the household and, at the same time, the line of descent in the family that includes ancestors. Under this system, the family head had the responsibility to manage the family property, arrange marriages for younger members of the family, supervise the family members and make sure that no one committed crimes or got into trouble, and maintained rituals for the ancestors. Under this system, all daughters were to be married out, one of the sons was to succeed the father as family head, and the rest of the sons had to either leave the family or become unmarried servants. Under the new civil law, this system was dismantled; however, the concept of family remains the fundamental source of identification of individuals in the society. It is revealed in the system of family registration.

THE HOUSEHOLD REGISTRATION SYSTEM

For a Japanese citizen, the most important basis for personal identification is an officially certified copy of his or her household register (*koseki*). When a child is born, the parents must register the child's name, date, and place of birth at the city hall. The newborn child's name is added to the register of the parents established at their marriage. For each newlywed couple, a new household register is created when the marriage is reported to the authorities. In the record, information is included about the couple's parents as well as the couple's own dates and places of birth. Whenever official identification is required (such as application for admission to a public school, registration for voting at elections, application for passport or driver's license), an individual must obtain an officially certified copy of the household register. Individuals may also be asked to produce copies when applying for jobs or getting married.

When a person dies, his or her name in the household register is crossed off, and the date of death is recorded. When a grown-up child gets married, his or her name is crossed off and information on the new register created by the marriage is written in. The household register for a Japanese national is just as important as the birth certificate is for an American citizen.

In the Japanese system, every child is assumed to be born to a married couple. The name of a child born out of wedlock is appended to the record of the mother, who is still registered as a member of her parents' household. If the father of the illegitimate child officially recognizes the child as his own, the name and address of the father are added to the record.

Marriage and divorce become official by filing reports at the city hall. No witness is required for marriage or divorce. No action at court is necessary if the divorce is based on mutual consent. Most divorces (about 90%) have been reported as "divorce by agreement" every year since revision of the Civil Code in 1947. When the divorce is reported, the name of the divorced woman is crossed off the household register that was established at the time of the marriage, and it is put back on the register of her parents with a note that her registration was transferred from her former husband's household.

This system of household registration was established during the Meiji era to support the traditional *ie* (family) system and to provide the government with information about individual subjects. The system was retained with some revision after World War II. The current system of establishing a new household register for every newlywed couple has been in practice since revision of the Civil Code in 1947.

The traditional Japanese family was the stem family with a single line of descent. The most important concerns were continuity of family line and integrity of family property. The family head was responsible for managing the family property, which was not to be divided. It was to be handed down to the next generation. The bride of the eldest son who was to be the family head was treated as the bride of the household, rather as the wife of the son. Her primary duty was to serve her parents-in-law, especially her mother-in-law, and care for them in their old age. If she failed to satisfy the parents-in-law, she could be divorced for the reason that she did not fit in the family.

After the war, the law of inheritance was revised and all children were entitled to equal inheritance. In many cases, however, the family house with the land beneath it is the major family property of the urban middle class today. One of the children and his or her family live with the parents in the family house with the understanding that they will look after the elderly parents.

The standard marriage in prewar days was arranged following the custom of *miai* (formal interview.) The family head and his wife, with the help of

Shinto wedding. Courtesy of Kyodo News.

relatives and family friends, looked around for a bride among women from households of roughly equal social standing as their own. They counted on a go-between (*nakoodo*) to arrange a formal interview with the prospective bride, bridegroom, and their parents. This interview could take place under the disguise of an accidental encounter at the theater or on an outing for cherry blossom viewing. Even if the family found a bride-to-be by themselves, it was necessary to have a go-between who would play the ritual role at the wedding ceremony and serve as mentor for the couple.

After the formal interview, if both families agreed to proceed, the young couple would be allowed to see each other before the wedding. If both parties agreed on engagement, the man's family would send a messenger to deliver a set of ceremonial gifts, called *yuino*, to the woman's family. The gift typically consisted of silk material for *kimono*, cash, *sake* (rice wine), and delicacies of the sea and land, which were placed on a lacquered tray. By accepting this gift the woman's parents expressed their consent to give their daughter to the man's family.

The traditional wedding took place at the man's house. In an upper-class samurai household, the bride was carried to the house on a sedan chair followed by the bearers of her dowry. Otherwise the bride came on horseback or on foot. The bride's costume varied in accordance with her social status.

One custom still observed today involves putting white headgear called *tsu-nokakushi* (literally, "concealment of the horns [of jealousy]") around the bride's head. All women were supposed to have horns grown out of jealousy. The hairdo of the bride reflected her marital status and age.

The wedding ceremony centered on the couple's sipping of rice wine. Three layers of short cups lacquered in bright red were placed on a tray. The bride and groom sipped the wine from the same cup. This ceremony is called "three, three, nine times" because both the bride and groom drank a cup of wine in three sips and repeated it three times, making a total of nine sips.

The ceremony was followed by a banquet. The typical main course was a grilled whole sea bream, which was shaped on the skewers so that its tail was pointed upward and the fish looked as if it were jumping. The red sea bream was regarded as a symbol of auspiciousness. In the course of the banquet, chanting of *utai* (chanted prose in the style of *noh* drama) took place. The most popular *utai* was from the noh drama entitled "Takasago." It is a story of an ancient couple who lived forever on the mysterious island of paradise.

POSTWAR CHANGES IN MARRIAGE CUSTOMS

After World War II, the traditional family system and marriage custom lost authority. The new type of marriage based on the young couple's choice was called "love marriage." Nevertheless, arranged marriage was regarded as more respectable. Because of the lack of a tradition of courtship in Japan, many failed cases of "love marriages" were reported and deplored. It was only after the marriage of Crown Prince Akihito (the Heisei emperor since 1989) and SHODA Michiko, the daughter of a businessman, in 1959 that "love marriage" was fully recognized as respectable. Empress Michiko was the first commoner to become the bride of a crown prince, and eventually she became empress. She met the crown prince as a tennis partner, and their marriage was reported to be a "love marriage."

For wedding ceremonies in Japan today, people choose from among Shinto, Christian, and nonreligious services, just as they choose bridal outfits from among traditional Japanese costume and Western-style wedding dress. The groom can wear either morning coat or formal silk kimono with the family crest on it. On top of the kimono, he would wear *haori* (a shorter outfit made of the same material as the kimono) and *hakama* (a kind of pleated outer skirt). Most men choose to wear a Western-style outfit.

Ceremony and reception are often held in a commercial wedding hall, which has chapels for Shinto, Christian, or nonreligious services, waiting rooms, reception halls, and dining hall complete with food service and other services. It is also popular to have the reception or banquet at a hotel. Couples who choose a religious ceremony hold it privately with family members and go-betweens. For most people, the religious ceremony is not as important as the social aspect of the wedding.

For the wedding banquet, a common pattern has developed. Guests are seated at the table following a carefully arranged seating order. Parents and close family members are seated in the back. After the guests are seated, the newlyweds enter the hall accompanied by the go-betweens, a successfully married older couple who will be models and counsels for the newlyweds. Most of the banquet is a series of toasts and speeches. Since the wedding is an important occasion for the young couple to confirm their social network, those who are important for their career (usually for the bridegroom's) are asked to give speeches. The speakers praise the talent and good character of the young man and the virtue of the bride, telling the assembled guests how respectable their families are. They craft their speeches to be entertaining. At one point, the bride withdraws from the dining hall accompanied by the go-between woman and reappears in a less formal and much brighter outfit. Some brides change their outfit more than once during the banquet. Toward the end of the banquet the newlyweds perform the ritual of slicing the wedding cake.

Commercial wedding halls thrive in Japan. Their advertisements are ubiquitous in commuter trains and subway stations. Even famous Shinto shrines run lucrative wedding hall businesses as a sideline.

Weddings in Japan today are quite expensive. Apart from the ceremony and banquet, the honeymoon trip has become standard, another custom adopted from the West. It is commonplace to go to Hawaii, Guam, or even Saipan. The cost of the wedding banquet is paid mostly by the family of the groom. In the traditional spirit of mutual help, invited guests are expected to bring a substantial amount of cash in a special gift envelope designed for weddings. The amount is determined by the social status of the guests and their relationship to the newlyweds. The Japanese have not adopted the American custom of giving a bridal shower or registering the "wish list" of gifts at department stores.

DIVORCE

In comparison with other industrialized countries (with the exception of Italy, a Catholic country), the divorce rate in postwar Japan has been low.[2] However, it has been rising, and the Japanese people in general have become much more accepting of divorce. According to a poll conducted by the Economic Planning Agency, almost 30 percent of respondents thought that troubled marriages should be ended as quickly as possible. This is quite a change from the attitude in the past when couples avoided divorcing for the sake of children, even if their own relationship had broken down. At the same time, remarriage of older men and women is no longer uncommon. Until about thirty years ago, divorced women generally had little desire to remarry. Today many actively seek another mate, reflecting changing expectations of the relationship between husband and wife.[3]

CHANGING CONCEPTS OF MARRIAGE AND FAMILY

Before 1947, two-thirds of marriages in Japan were arranged. In the latter half of the 1960s, the proportion dropped to less than half. According to a government survey in 1997, only 9.6 percent of the couples who married between 1992 and 1997 considered their marriages as arranged. Of those who were united by "love marriage," most met each other at work (33.6%), through the introduction of friends or siblings (27.1%), or at school (10.4%). According to the same survey, the average length of courtship was 3.4 years, and the average age of the women at their first marriage was 26.1 years. This is somewhat higher than the average age of women at their first marriage in the United States.[4]

A growing number of men and women in Japan are putting off marriage until their late twenties. In 1992, the average age of marriage was 28.4 for first-time grooms and 26.0 for first-time brides. It has been a trend among Japanese women to marry late and to have fewer children, if any. When the government announced in 1990 that the total fertility rate (overall number of children born to women in their childbearing years) had dropped to 1.57, this news shocked the nation, because it means that the population of Japan is on the decline and that the proportion of the elderly has greatly increased in the total population.

Another fact revealed in the 1990 census which startled the public was the increase of the proportion of men and women who had never married. Fully 11.7 percent of men between age 40 and 44, and 13.9 percent of women between age 30 and 34, were reported to have never married. Over 4 percent of men and women between age 50 and 54 were never married. Because more women now earn enough to support themselves, they do not have to resort to marriage as a means of financial security. This fact makes them less willing to marry someone who does not meet their expectations. Besides, housework and child rearing are still mostly left to women despite the fact that more men are willing to share the responsibility than before.

NOTES

1. *Japan: A Pocket Guide*, 1996 ed. (Tokyo: Foreign Press Center, 1996), p. 149.

2. The number of divorced couples per 1,000 population during 1991 was 1.3 in Japan, 2.9 in Britain, 1.9 in France, 3.1 in Canada, and 4.7 in the United States. See Mori Takashi, ed., Kokuseisha, *Sekai kokusei zue*, (Illustrated statistics of the world) 1994–1995 ed. (Tokyo: Kokuseisha, 1993), p. 456.

3. Yasuhiko Yuzawa, *Japanese Families*, About Japan Series, no. 19 (Tokyo: Foreign Press Center, 1994), pp. 30–32.

4. *Yomiuri shimbun*, June 7, 1998.

9

Holidays, Festivals, and Annual Events

Many holidays and festivals in Japan have their origins in tradition. Because rice cultivation was the mainstream way of life in preindustrial Japan, many festivals are related to the annual cycle of planting, growing, and harvesting, which followed the four seasons. Festivals and holidays were observed when a major task in rice cultivation was completed. They gave rhythm to life in a village community. During festivals, people took a break from their work to rest and engage in recreational activities. It was a time not only for recuperation from hard work but also for communal activities to enhance harmony in the community.

In the modern age, fewer traditional holidays and festivals are observed. Even if they are, they are not necessarily celebrated in the traditional ways. Today, the most important holidays are New Years Day and the Mid-Summer Buddhist festival. During these holiday seasons, many urban residents return to their former homes in the countryside. A large proportion of the population of metropolitan areas have rural roots, their families having lived in the cities only for two or three generations. During the New Year and Mid-Summer seasons, many return to visit relatives who have stayed in the rural areas and to participate in family rituals for their ancestors. A massive exodus takes place from every large city, especially from Tokyo, causing extreme congestion on highways and overcrowding of public transportation systems.

In recent decades, some of the old festivals have been promoted to attract tourists to boost local commercial interests. The tourism industry is indeed very important in Japan. After the country achieved economic prosperity, tourism became a popular activity among young people as well as retired people and owners of small businesses who have flexible time. Local festivals with some distinction serve as a perfect attraction for tourists. Many festivals in various areas of Japan are covered on television and thereby attract an even greater number of visitors.

Following are some of the most commonly observed holidays and nationally well-known festivals in local communities all over Japan. The descriptions of activities relate to contemporary Japan. Many traditional customs related to holidays and festivals are not only simplified but also standardized in the modern era. Moreover, their dates have been modified since Japan adopted Gregorian calendar in place of the traditional lunar calendar in 1872. Until around the 1950s, however, people in rural areas continued to observe lunar calendar dates for unofficial celebrations. Some people even celebrated twice, following both the old and new calendars. In recent years, however, the dates have followed the official calendar even though lunar dates make more sense because they reflect changes in the seasons. For example, on New Years Day one traditionally celebrates the coming of early spring. It falls in mid or late February according to the lunar calendar. The first day of the year in the Gregorian calendar comes in the midst of winter and a bit too soon for early spring, but people still greet each other expressing best wishes for the new spring as well as for the new year.

THE NEW YEAR

The New Year is celebrated by everyone and is taken more seriously than any other holiday. It punctuates life in Japan by marking the beginning of an annual cycle.

While trying to get ready for the New Year, people become increasingly frantic toward the end of the last month of the year, whose poetic name is *shiwasu* (the month when even [dignified] teachers run about). They are anxious to get all sorts of work done so they don't have to carry it over to the new year. Department stores and other commercial establishments heighten the frenzy by advertising end-of-the-year bargain sales.

December is the major season for gift-giving, or *oseibo*. It is a time to fulfill social obligations by expressing gratitude to those whom one is indebted to. Most commonly, the gift is sent to one's relatives, business associates, and immediate superiors at the work place. The value of the gifts varies, but most are drinks (ranging from expensive liquor to soft drinks and tea) and food (such as dried seaweed, canned food, preserved food, and fruits). Department stores set up special gift sections to help shoppers select appropriate items and to deliver them. This kind of gift-giving takes two times a year, at the end of the year and at mid-summer. At each season it is customary for government and private organizations to pay their employees a bonus. Normally, the amount paid in December is higher than that paid in mid-year.

To start the new year with a clean slate, all debts and obligations due by the year's end must be cleared. Dust that accumulated during the year inside and around the house must be cleaned away so that every place is spic-and-span by New Years morning. For those who live in Japanese-style houses, the year-end housecleaning is a major family event that involves removing dust from the ceilings and beams, lifting the heavy *tatami* mats from floors of all the rooms for airing and dusting, replacing translucent paper on the *shoji* (sliding doors) inside the house, and cleaning nooks and corners. Some people may not be so thorough, but they do their best in their own ways. Even residential streets are impeccably cleaned by those who live in the neighborhood.

After the cleaning, New Years decorations are placed in and around the house. On the gate of the house, a pair of *kadomatsu* (pine branches for New Year) are placed. Sometimes plum and bamboo are added. Inside the house, the *kamidana* (altar of gods) is decorated with *shimenawa* (a sacred straw rope with folded paper strips hanging from it) and *kagami-mochi* (round mirror-shaped rice cakes). On the *tokonoma* alcove of the main parlor, a flower arrangement enhances the New Years atmosphere.

Preparation for the New Years feast, *osechi ryori*, must be completed by New Years Eve so that cooking does not occur for the first three days of the New Years celebration. *Osechi ryori* originally referred to dishes for ceremonies prepared as offerings to gods. Not only at New Years, ceremonies in every season constituted an important part of the life of aristocrats in ancient Japan, who elaborated the ritual, food, and costume for each ceremony. Certain ancient aristocratic customs spread among the commoners during the Edo period and continue to this day. Osechi ryori is aesthetically arranged in four or five lacquer boxes, called *jubako*, stacked on top of each other. It includes pickled herring roe, grilled fish, dried anchovies cooked in sweet sauce, red and white fish cakes, black soybeans, mashed chestnuts, radishes, burdock, kumquats, lotus roots, shiitake mushrooms, and ginko nuts. Each has a symbolic meaning to facilitate good health or good luck. These used to be considered special treats; however, the Japanese taste—especially that of the younger generation—changed after being exposed to gourmet food from all over the world. Nevertheless, osechi ryori is becoming popular again.

Osechi ryori: New Year's feast. Courtesy of Kyodo News.

One reason is because department stores sell pre-ordered boxes of it, which saves time for people who do not have time or know-how to prepare it.

The late-night snack for New Years Eve is *soba* (buckwheat noodle). It is simple to prepare and takes little time to eat—just dip the boiled noodle in soy sauce-based soup and briskly slurp. This "fast food" of the old days is delivered to homes at no extra charge. Since everyone is extremely busy on New Years Eve trying to finish every last chore of the year, soba is the most convenient food.

At midnight on New Years Eve, every Buddhist temple strikes its heavy bronze bell. The sound travels deep and far, resonating as though it is swelling from the depths of the ground. The bell is struck 108 times on the belief that every human being has 108 kinds of worldly desires that cause suffering. Each sound of the bell is meant to strike out each of the desires.

In the early morning hours, Shinto shrines begin to be crowded with worshippers. Those who stayed home try to get up early enough to worship at the first rising sun of the new year. Those who disregard conventionalism and stay in bed enjoy "sleeping New Year." Others, following recent vogue, travel abroad during the New Years season.

The New Years ceremony at home is centered on drinking herb-seasoned *sake* and eating *o-zoni*, a piece of rice cake in clear soup. The soup is prepared in various ways according to local tradition. Children receive *o-toshidama* (New Years small money gift) from their parents. It is meant to be a gift from the tutelary god. With blessing of the god, everyone gains another year to add to one's age. According to the traditional method of reckoning, everyone adds a year to one's age on New Years Day, not on one's birthday. Thus even a baby born on the last day of the last month of the year becomes a "second-year child" on New Years Day and is regarded to be 2 years old.

Everything one does on New Years Day is important because one tends to repeat the same thing for the rest of the year. That's why everyone wants to have a happy, healthy, harmonious New Years Day. Even the New Years dream is important, and everyone hopes to have a dream with good omen.

Traditionally, the second day of the year is for ritual beginning of work. For those who use writing brushes in their work, it is the day for *kakizome* (first writing of the year). For schoolchildren, brush-writing for the new year is still practiced as an annual event at schools, but not quite on the second day of the year. On the actual second day, schools hold a brief ceremony in the auditorium where teachers and students gather in their New Years dress. At work places, workers used to show up in their New Years outfits to greet their bosses and each other on this ritual first day of work. Nowadays, the ritual takes place on the morning of the first day of the real work week. Workers show up in more or less formal attire and exchange greetings, saying, "Happy New Year!" and "Thank you for your collegiality last year; please be the same this year."

For the first three days of the New Year, government offices, private companies, and schools are closed to allow everyone to celebrate. The first seven days of the year, when the *kadomatsu* are kept on the household gates, are regarded as the period of celebration. During this time, people make formal calls on relatives, superiors at work, and anyone to whom one owes a formal expression of indebtedness. For such visits and for trips to shrines and temples during the New Years season, many women don traditional *kimono* with long sleeves and broad sash. This is the only time of the year when many women in kimono are seen on streets and in public transportation systems.

New Years cards (*nengajo*) were originally substitutes for personal visits for New Years greetings. Nowadays, people send many cards. An average Japanese may even send more New Years cards than an average American sends season's greetings cards! Many people send custom-made printed cards with-

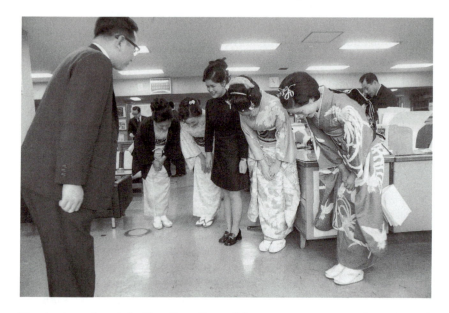

First business day of the New Year. Four of the women are wearing the traditional *kimono*. Courtesy of Kyodo News.

out adding any handwritten message. Unlike a Christmas card, which is normally put in an envelope, a New Years card is always written on a post-card. Those mailed during the designated period in December are stored at the post office, and all are delivered on New Years Day. It is not proper to deliver them before New Years Day, because the customary phrases express congratulations on having had a happy New Year (the day itself, not the coming year).

Those who had a death in the family during the past year are not supposed to join the celebration of the new year. Earlier in December they notify friends and associates, explaining what happened to the family and apolo-gizing for not sending New Years cards.

Traditional games for children are played during the New Years season. Boys fly kites, spin tops, and ride bamboo horses. Girls play Japanese battle-dore (Japanese badminton) with elaborately decorated wooden paddles. Girls used to play it in long-sleeved kimono.

Popular indoor games for New Years are card games, such as *i-ro-ha karuta* (cards for learning characters) for children, *hana-fuda* (flower cards), and cards commonly used in the United States and elsewhere (called "trump" in Japan). The most representative New Years card game is *hyakunin-isshu*, involving one hundred poems compiled in the thirteenth century. Two sets of 100 cards are used. On each card in the first set, a poem is printed. The type of poem is known as *waka* with 31 syllables written in five lines: 5, 7, 5, 7, 7 syllables in each line. The cards in the second set, with beautiful brush writing of only the last two lines of a poem, are placed on the floor face-up. A number of people sit around the cards, listen to one person read out the poem from the first set of cards, and try to pick up the matching card from the floor. The winner is the one who picks the most cards. Those who have memorized many of the poems can pick up the card very quickly. An expert is able to identify the correct card as soon as the first syllable of the poem has been read. This game helps maintain the tradition of classic poetry among Japanese young people.

At the imperial household, the tradition of classic poetry is taken very seriously. During the New Years season, a ceremony to mark the beginning of poem writing and reading in the new year takes place. Not only do members of the imperial family present their poems to be read, but the general public is also invited to present poems. Those who are selected are invited to the ceremony at the imperial palace. A topic is announced early in the previous year, and a committee selects winners from poems sent from all over the country or abroad. This ceremony is in the spirit of the ancient anthology, *Man'yoshu*, which was compiled in the eighth century under imperial auspices.

BON (MID-SUMMER FESTIVAL)

Bon (Mid-Summer Buddhist festival, or ghost festival), the second biggest holiday, is another occasion for mass migration of urban residents to mid-year family reunions at their old homes in the countryside. The custom of sending a mid-summer gift, or *o-chugen*, to express a debt of gratitude is very similar to that of *o-seibo* at the end of the year. Also, hot summer is another season at which to send greeting cards to inquire after the health and well-being of friends and associates. Mid-summer greeting cards, or *shochu mimai*, can be sent at any time throughout the summer after the rainy season (from mid-June through mid-July) is over; however, people do not send as many mid-summer cards as they send New Years cards.

Traditionally the Bon festival was from the 13th through the 15th of the lunar seventh month. Nowadays, it is observed from July 13 through 15 in most places in Japan. In some areas it is observed from August 13 through 15. According to tradition, the spirits of ancestors come home during this period. To prepare for the reunion with them, people go to the family graveyard to clean the tombstones. On the evening of the 13th they build a bonfire at the front gate of the house and light lanterns around the family altar. During the three-day period the family offers specially prepared vegetarian feasts at the altar, ideally on a placemat freshly woven of fragrant water grass. During the Tokugawa period, it was customary to give live-in servants and workshop employees a leave to go home for the Bon festival. It was believed that even the lid of hell was opened in order to let the devils in charge take a break. This meant that many hungry ghosts who had no family to feed them would roam around the street, so people would set a separate table for them. It was an important act of charity to feed the beggars, either alive or dead. Some families, especially those who lost a member to death during the past year, invite a Buddhist priest for sutra chanting. Thus Buddhist priests are often seen on streets and public transportation in their black robes, responding to house calls.

At the end of the three-day homecoming, the ancestors' spirits are supposed to return to the Buddhist paradise located beyond the western border of this world. To send them off, people used to set out a take-home gift of food on a small boat. Instead of building a boat, many people placed food on a lotus leaf and floated it on a river. This custom, known as *shoro nagashi*, can no longer be practiced because of environmental regulations. To mark the end of the Bon festival and the mid-summer season, neighborhood communities organize *Bon odori* (Bon dancing). To folk songs accompanied by drum and flute, men and women in *yukata* (cotton summer *kimono*) with oval fans in their hands dance in a circle on a blocked-off street.

Between the New Years and the Mid-Summer festival, several other holidays traditionally served as markers of seasons. The following are some of the holidays that are still observed more or less seriously.

SETSUBUN (CELEBRATION OF NEW SEASON)

In ancient times, rituals to commemorate passage of the four seasons were observed at the imperial court. For the court nobles and aristocrats during the Heian period, these were very serious concerns. Celebration of the beginning of spring, the most important ritual, had spread among the commoners by the Tokugawa period and became nationally observed. It is not designated as a national holiday, and the custom is no longer observed in most households. But it is kept in some Buddhist temples, where many people gather to participate in ceremonies.

On the eve of *risshun* (the beginning of spring, which falls on February 3 or 4), a ritual took place in the imperial court in ancient times to chase out evil spirits. Later, ordinary people adopted the ritual of scattering beans inside their house while shouting "Devils out, Fortune in!" For children, it is fun to scatter beans wearing homemade masks of the devil or goddess of fortune. During the postwar period when sweets were scarce, the treat of roasted soybeans made this ritual doubly fun.

SPRING AND AUTUMN EQUINOXES

Spring and Autumn Equinoxes used to be remembered as *higan*, meaning "the other side of the river," or "the realm of the departed souls." Buddhist memorial services took place at this time. On and around those days, families visited ancestral tombs to clean the tombstones and offered sweet rice balls covered with sweet red beans or roasted sesame at their family altars. Even today, for many people the equinoxes are days for visiting ancestral tombs.

DOLL FESTIVAL, OR PEACH BLOSSOM FESTIVAL

The Doll festival falls on the third day of the third month. In ancient times when this festival for girls started, dolls were made of straw or paper as objects of ritual exorcism. In the ritual, evils attached to women were transferred to the dolls, which were set adrift on a river. Nowadays, the festival celebrates the growth of girls. For this day, girls get a set of elaborately manufactured dolls representing ancient court nobles and accompanying ornaments. They are displayed at home on a terraced stage covered with red cloth. Branches of peach blossoms are part of the decoration. To celebrate, girls get together in their *kimono* to play traditional girls' games such as *o-tedama* (juggling balls made of soft cloth with loosely packed beans in them) and *mari-tsuki* (bouncing balls). Sweet white *sake*, diamond-shaped rice cakes, and rice crackers are customarily served. After the celebration, the dolls are stored away until the following year.

HANAMI (CHERRY BLOSSOM VIEWING)

The Japanese have a passion for cherry blossoms, which symbolized ultimate beauty in literature from ancient times. When cherry blossoms come to bloom, it is the beginning of the balmy spring season. People love to picnic under cherry trees in full bloom, enjoying *sake* and special lunch boxes under the blossoms that spread like a heavenly tent. The flowers do not last long. No sooner do they come to full bloom than they begin to shed their petals like snowflakes. When cherry blossom time approaches, people become anxious to know which day is the best for *hanami*. The national weather

Hanami: cherry blossom viewing parties at Ueno Park. Courtesy of Kyodo News.

bureau reports the progress of cherry blossoms day by day, as the peak starts in Okinawa and moves northward to Hokkaido. Radio and television stations report every day on the conditions of blossoms at areas in peak season.

Famous sites of cherry blossoms are very crowded with people. In public parks with cherry trees, such as Ueno Park in Tokyo, some people stay overnight before their *hanami* party to secure a spot under the cherry blossoms. The view of Mt. Yoshino in Nara prefecture, where the entire mountain is covered with cherry trees from bottom to top, has been regarded as the best in Japan since ancient times.

Hana Matsuri (Floral Festival), or Buddha's Birthday

April 8 is regarded as Buddha's birthday. At Buddhist temples, a small image of the Buddha is placed in a specially constructed basin in front of the temple building. People come to pour *amacha* (sweet tea) over the statue.

Tango-No-Sekku

May 5 has been designated as a national holiday, Children's Day. Traditionally, it was a boy's festival. Wishing their sons to grow up to be strong and courageous men, families with boys fly carp streamers and hang iris and herbs on the eaves of their houses. These plants were believed to protect people against evil spirits. Inside the house, families display warrior dolls and decorative helmets of the feudal age. Special food for this day is *chimaki* (*zongzi* in Chinese), sweet rice steamed in broad bamboo leaves with seasoned meat or sweet bean paste mixed with walnuts. Another food associated with this day is *kashiwa mochi*, a dumpling made of rice flour with sweet bean paste inside and steamed in an oak leaf. Celebration of the fifth day of the lunar fifth month originated in ancient China to commemorate a patriotic but disfavored minister.

NATSU-MATSURI (SUMMER FESTIVALS), *AKI-MATSURI* (AUTUMN FESTIVALS), *HARU-MATSURI* (SPRING FESTIVALS), AND *FUYU-MATSURI* (WINTER FESTIVALS)

Every Shinto shrine has its own day for an annual or seasonal festival. (See also "Shinto" in the section on Religion in Chapter 2.) Traditionally, festivals in farming communities were tied to the agricultural work schedule. They took place before or after the major work seasons. In the early spring, a festival served as a celebration for the beginning of the planting season. During the growing season in the summer, villagers offered prayers for normal growth of crops. The late autumn festival was to offer a thanksgiving feast for the new crops. In the past when farming was the main occupation of most everyone in Japan, every village participated in the autumn harvest festival. Many villages held processions of tall banners with music ensembles of drum and flute, or even with masked dancers. Nowadays, because of the industrialization and urbanization of Japanese life, the population in the countryside and in most villages has been reduced, and there are not enough young people to carry out traditional activities for the festival. Nevertheless, some local communities have maintained the tradition as a strategy for economic development and to attract tourists from all over the country.

Many festivals at urban shrines take place during the summer. Most originally involved praying for protection from epidemic disease, which was a serious problem in cities in pre-modern times. During the festival, common features include lighting lanterns at the entrance of individual houses, procession of portable shrines and bands of drums and flute, building bonfires, and holding various food and flower fairs. Many nationally well known festivals attract tourists. These include festivals listed below.

AOI MATSURI (Hollyhock festival) of Shimogamo and Kamigamo shrines in Kyoto. The festival features a colorful pageant reproducing the imperial procession that paid homage to these shrines in the ancient past. (May 15)

SANJA MATSURI (Asakusa shrine festival) in Asakusa district of Tokyo. A festival to celebrate the arrival of summer. From shrines in old downtown districts *mikoshi* (portable shrines) are carried out by men and women, and altogether almost one hundred of them assemble at the Asakusa shrine. They then parade to their respective parishioners' areas. (Weekend around May 18)

CHAGU-CHAGU UMAKO (Horse festival) in Morioka, Iwate prefecture. This festival is observed to offer prayers to Sozen shrine for the health of horses. Colorfully decorated horses are led by their proud owners to the shrine in procession. (June 15)

TANABABA MATSURI (Star festival) is based on Chinese legend. On the seventh day of the seventh month, the stars Vega and her lover ox-herd, Altair, are allowed to meet across the Milky Way. Since Vega was an excellent weaver, women used to set up bamboo branches on which to tie strips of paper with their prayer wishes to the star. Later it became a festival of children. More recently, it has become a great display of decoration in the commercial districts of cities. Of these, the decorations in Sendai are the most elaborate. (July 7)

GION MATSURI (Gion festival) of Yasaka shrine in Kyoto. One of the grandest festivals in Kyoto, it is celebrated from July 1 through 31, centering on July 17 and 18, when parades with festival music take place all night. It dates back to the ninth century when the priest of the Yasaka shrine led a procession of many men and women to seek the gods' protection against pestilence that was ravaging the city. (July 17–18)

NEBUTA MATSURI (Nebuta festival) in Aomori. Enormous floats representing ancient warrior-heroes, animals, and birds are paraded and at the end of the festival are floated in streams. This celebrates the summer and prepares for the Mid-Summer Bon festival. (August 1–7)

OKUNCHI (festival of Suwa shrine) in Nagasaki. This is of Chinese origin because there was a Chinese community in Nagasaki during the Tokugawa period. A Chinese-style parade with dance takes place. (October 7–9)

JIDAI MATSURI (Festival of Eras) at Heian shrine in Kyoto. This commemorates the founding of the old capital city, Heian-kyo, in present-day Kyoto in 794. A procession of over 2,000 people dressed in traditional costumes representing important epochs in the city's history takes place. (October 22)

MOON-VIEWING FESTIVAL

This takes place in the evening of the full moon of the lunar eighth month ("the harvest moon" in America). The custom is to offer rice dumplings to the moon along with an arrangement of autumn flowers, and to share them with family and friends while viewing the full moon—ideally on an outdoor deck. This festival originated in China, where extended family members get together to confirm their harmony over a feast. In Japan, Chinese-style moon cakes, with sweet bean paste and lotus seeds and chestnuts inside, are sold in department stores and regarded as delicacies. However, the Japanese do not regard this festival as an important occasion for family gatherings. In Japan, it is another occasion to enjoy communion with nature.

SHICHI-GO-SAN

Shichi-go-san literally means "seven, five, three." On November 15, parents dress up boys at age 3 and 5 and girls at age 3 and 7 (by the Japanese reckoning of age) and take them to a Shinto shrine to report that they have reached the given age and to ask for divine protection. This originated from rites of passage among samurai of the Edo period. Now, it is a day for young families to lavishly dress up their children in traditional costume and take their pictures at a Shinto shrine. The standard accessory of the day is a two-foot-long bag of *Chitose-ame* ("thousand-year" candy), a wish for long life.

NIINAME-SAI (THANKSGIVING FOR NEW CROPS) OR *KINRO KANSHA-NO-HI* (LABOR THANKSGIVING DAY)

Thanksgiving for New Crops on November 23 is a ritual at Shinto shrines. Originally it was a ritual at the imperial palace, where the emperor offered to the gods of heaven and earth samples of crops harvested from the sacred field. It has been one of the religious duties of the emperor to perform rituals to invoke divine protection at each stage of the growing season at the sacred field, where he personally plants and harvests rice. As a national holiday, this day is officially established as KINRO-KANSHA-NO-HI (Labor Thanksgiving Day).

NATIONAL HOLIDAYS

New Years Day, as well as Spring and Autumn Equinoxes, are designated as official national holidays. The rest of the numerous holidays are either not officially observed as national holidays or have been given new interpretations.

When the national holidays were instituted after World War II, their original religious implications were eliminated from the official descriptions. The following days are designated as national holidays when government offices, schools, and companies are closed:

- January 1: New Years Day. Celebrates the beginning of the new year.

- January 15: Coming of Age Day. Celebrates the coming of age of young men and women who have turned 20. Those who are 20 years old have voting rights.

- February 11: National Foundation Day. According to legend, the first emperor of Japan ascended to the throne on this day in the year 660 B.C.

- March 21 or 22: Spring Equinox Day. A day for praising nature and showing love of all living things.

- April 29: Greenery Day. Commemorates the Showa emperor's love for living creatures in nature and the many trees he planted on tours throughout the country. Until 1988, this day was celebrated as the emperor's birthday.

- May 3: Constitution Memorial Day. Commemorates the day on which the New Constitution came into effect in 1947.

- May 4 (if it falls between Monday and Friday): Holiday for a Nation. Designated as a holiday in the 1990s simply because it falls in between two national holidays, so that people can have a continuous three-day holiday.

- May 5: Children's Day. Wishes are expressed that children will grow up in good health and find happiness.

- July 20: Marine Day. A new holiday created recently, this is the first day of summer vacation for most schools in Japan. Summer vacation was always associated with going to ocean beaches.

- September 15: Respect for the Aged Day. A day for showing respect and affection for the elderly, who have devoted themselves to society for many years, and for celebrating their long life. In cities, towns, and villages, the elderly are invited to entertainments and receive gifts to mark the occasion.

- September 23 or 24: Autumn Equinox. Ancestors are honored, and the deceased are remembered.
- October 10: Health and Sports Day. Commemorates the 1964 Tokyo Olympiad, the opening ceremony of which took place on October 10. Many sporting events are held on this day.
- November 3: National Culture Day. A day for celebrating freedom and equality, and for promoting culture; commemorates promulgation of the New Constitution on November 3, 1946. Before 1945, this day was celebrated as the birthday of the Meiji emperor.
- November 23: Labor Thanksgiving Day. Traditional thanksgiving day at Shinto shrines.
- December 23: Emperor's Birthday. The Heisei emperor was born on December 23, 1933.

10

Leisure Activities and Entertainment

According to a public opinion survey conducted by the prime minister's office in 1995, leisure and leisure activities are becoming increasingly important for people in Japan.[1] When asked about their priorities, 35.3 percent considered leisure and leisure activities a top priority, compared to 18.1 percent in 1976. In both years, this category was followed by housing, eating, durable consumer goods, and clothing. Among the top ten leisure activities were special dining-out, driving, domestic travel (to hot springs and other places), *karaoke*, watching videos, going to bars and snack bars, listening to recorded music, going to amusement parks, and bowling. These were followed by playing the lottery, playing cards, picnicking and walking, gardening, getting physical exercise, going to movie theaters, watching TV games, playing *pachinko* (a type of pinball), going to events and exhibitions, and ocean bathing.

The cost of leisure activities varies a great deal. Among the most expensive, the most popular activities in 1995 involved overseas travel, golf, yachts and motor boats, hostess bars, personal computer communication, domestic travel, and surfing. The most popular among the less expensive activities involved playing *shogi* (Japanese chess) at clubs, playing cards, basketball, physical exercise, softball, jogging, and volleyball.

Categories of leisure activities with the most participants are, in order, as follows: bowling, physical exercise, jogging, swimming, fishing, and playing catch and baseball. Categories of hobbies and creative activities with the most participants are, in order, as follows: watching videos, listening to recorded

Downtown street near the train station. Courtesy of Noriko Kamachi.

music, gardening, going to movies, going to concerts, and watching sports in person. In the amusement category, the following are most popular: special dining-out, *karaoke*, bars, lottery, playing cards, and *pachinko*; in tourism and travel: driving, domestic travel, zoos (and aquariums, etc.), amusement parks, picnicking and walking, and ocean bathing. In gambling, the overwhelming leader is central government–sponsored horse racing; this is followed by local government–sponsored horse racing, speedboat racing, bicycle racing, and auto racing.

PACHINKO

Pachinko is a kind of vertical pinball game. Pachinko parlors with tens or even hundreds of machines are ubiquitous in downtown areas all over Japan. Formerly an inexpensive pastime, the game offered prizes of a pack of cigarettes or a candy box. Now a large amount of money is involved, and people can gain or lose as much as one hundred thousand yen (roughly $1,000). Since cash prizes are prohibited, the winners get tickets for cigarettes and other goods; however, tickets can be exchanged for cash at nearby stores.

Pachinko parlor. Courtesy of Kyodo News.

KARAOKE

Singing to *karaoke* (literally, "empty orchestra"), or recorded accompaniment music, at karaoke bars has become very popular in Japan since the 1970s, and now it has spread to other Asian countries and beyond.

In early years, heavy karaoke machines equipped with recording tapes and microphones were installed in hostess bars for after-hours entertainment. There the customers took turns with the microphone, singing for the entire room. The selection of songs ranged from World War II military songs to *enka* ballads (songs in vogue during the 1950s). The customers were mostly middle-aged salarymen. During the 1980s compact and laser discs were introduced, and "karaoke boxes," sound-proofed private rooms for small groups or individuals, appeared. Thereafter karaoke gained enormous popularity among the younger generations and women, and became a mainstream popular entertainment. The selection of songs expanded to include all sorts of new songs including foreign songs known to the Japanese. Today karaoke on-line service systems send songs over telephone wires to clubs and home karaoke systems on demand. Karaoke systems at clubs have added a visual dimension, creating fantasies of singing in romantic scenery. A virtual karaoke system with electronic instruments allows singers to perform in fa-

Sumo wrestlers: Akebono (right) versus Taka-no-Nami. Courtesy of Kyodo News.

mous concert halls of their choice or even to design their own concert halls with the desired sound effect. In addition, many schools across the country have karaoke equipment in their music rooms where kids can sing along to professionally produced video music and images on large screens.

SUMO

Sumo and baseball are the most popular spectator sports in Japan. *Sumo* is a special type of wrestling of ancient origin. It has been a professional spectator sport for almost 300 years and is now practiced in high schools, colleges, and amateur associations. A wrestler wins by forcing his opponent out of the center of the circle or by causing him to touch the surface of the *dohyo* (ring) with any part of his body other than the soles of his feet. The sumo match is filled with rituals, and the referee is dressed in the style of an ancient court nobleman. Six annual tournaments of Grand Sumo are exclusively broadcast by NHK (Nippon Hoso Kyokai, or Japan Broadcasting Company). At each tournament, the ranking of wrestlers is determined by their record. *Yokozuna*, the grand champion, is at the top of the pyramid-like ranking system of the wrestlers.

Shogi (chess) players' club. Courtesy of
Kyodo News.

MARTIAL ARTS

Practicing martial arts such as *kendo* (fencing with bamboo swords), *judo*, *karate, aikido,* or *kyudo* (Japanese archery) is a popular leisure activity.

GAMBLING

Gambling on horse racing, speedboat racing, motorbike racing, and bicycle racing is sponsored by the central or local government. Public lotteries are also sponsored by the government. Any gambling not backed by local or central government is illegal in Japan.

GO, SHOGI, MAHJONG

These are the most popular indoor games. *Go* is played by two players with black and white stones on a 19-by-19 grid board with 361 intersections. The players take turns placing stones on intersections to enclose a territory, and the one who captures the most territory wins.

Shogi is the Japanese version of chess. Instead of figurines, flat wooden chips with Chinese characters representing kings, generals, and soldiers are used.

Both *go* and *shogi* were transmitted from China in ancient times. They were played by aristocrats in the Heian period but later became popular across the social strata. National championship tournaments with professional players are televised, and the champions are highly respected.

Mahjong is a relatively new Chinese game introduced to Japan in the twentieth century. Four players at the table play with 136 tiles of ivory or bamboo.

CINEMA

"Motion pictures" (*katsudo shashin*), as they were called in early years, first appeared in Japan in 1896 when Thomas Edison's peepshow Kinetoscope was imported. By 1900 the Japanese were filming scenarios and stage performances of their own. The first dramas in motion pictures were brief excerpts of plays performed by stage actors of kabuki or modern theater. From this time on, two major categories of Japanese movies have been *jidai-geki* (period drama), whose setting is in the historical past, and *gendai-geki* (modern drama). Many modern dramas performed in the early years on stage or on screen were Japanese adaptations of European novels and dramas.

During the 1920s a popular culture based on the urban middle class flourished. The images of fashionable "modern girls" in Western dress sitting at a coffee shop where imported records were played represented the new urban culture in the post–World War I era. Imported movies became a part of this modern culture. The first serious Japanese movie drama with editing appeared in 1919. MIZOGUCHI Kenji (1898–1956), KINUGAWA Teinosuke (1896–1982), OZU Yasujiro (1903–1963), and NARUSE Mikio (1905–1969) began to make movies in the 1920s and remained influential directors in later years.

Before the "talkie" became successful in the 1930s, silent movies encoding imported movies were shown in Japanese theaters with a live performer called *benshi* (narrator) or *katsuben* (narrator of *katsudo shashin*). He sat by the side of the screen in full view of the audience and provided narrative details and his own interpretations and didactic comments. The benshi's performance, accompanied by traditional *shamisen* or Western musical instruments, was in the same fashion as the *joruri* chanting of traditional puppet theater, and itself became a major attraction at movie theaters.

After the era of repression under the military-dominated government during the 1930s and 1940s, Japanese cinema entered a creative golden age during the 1950s. In 1951 *Rashomon*, a *jidai-geki* of KUROSAWA Akira (1910–1998), won at the Venice Film Festival, and thereafter Japanese films became known to international audiences. Kurosawa continued to produce jidai-geki such as *Shichinin no samurai* (Seven Samurai, 1954), *Yojimbo* (1961), and *Tsubaki Sanjuro* (1962), as well as modern dramas about social issues such as *Ikiru* (To Live, 1952), *Warui yatsu hodo yoku nemuru* (The Bad Sleep Well, 1960), and *Tengoku to jigoku* (High and Low, 1963). Kurosawa also produced adaptations of Shakespearean and other foreign drama. *Kumonosujo* (The Throne of Blood, 1957) is a Japanese adaptation of "Macbeth." Kurosawa remained prolific into his eighties. Actor MIFUNE Toshiro (d. 1997) performed the hero's role in many of Kurosawa's films.

Kurosawa was not alone in gaining international recognition for Japanese cinema. MIZOGUCHI Kenji, who directed *Ugetsu Monogatari* (1953), OZU Yasujiro, NARUSE Mikio, KINOSHITA Keisuke (1912–), ICHIKAWA Kon (1915–), and others competed with each other. Among younger-generation directors who earned acclaimed international reputations, there are: IMAMURA Shohei (1926–), who directed *Unagi* (Eel), a winner at the Cannes International Film Festival of 1997; TESHIGAHARA Hiroshi (1927–), director of *Suna no onna* (Woman in the Dunes, 1964); SHINODA Masahiro (1931–), director of *Shinju ten no Amijima* (Love Suicide at Amijima, 1969); OSHIMA Nagisa (1932–), *Ai no Korida* (Realm of the Senses, 1976); ITAMI Juzo (1933–1997), *Tampopo* (1985); and SUO Masayuki, whose *Shall We Dance* (1996) expresses the sentiment of white-collar workers in post-affluence Tokyo. The greatest success at box offices and in critics' reviews in the recent past was a series of films, *Otoko wa tsurai yo* (It's Tough Being a Man, 1969–1996), directed by YAMADA Yoji (1931–). The hero in the series, Tora-san, was played by ATSUMI Kiyoshi (1928–1996). By the time of Atsumi's death, over forty films had been released.

MANGA (COMICS) AND ANIMATED PICTURES

One of the most remarkable phenomena in Japanese culture is the explosive popularity of comic books and comic magazines since the 1970s. About one-third of the books and magazines published in the mid-1990s are *manga*, that is, publications solely dedicated to cartoons and comic strips. More than fifty comic magazines for youths and adults are published weekly, biweekly, or monthly, and most issues have more than two hundred pages. There are comic magazines for youth, for adults, for boys, and for girls. All types contain about ten or more serialized stories, some with contents that are extremely violent or almost pornographic. Foreigners touring in Japan may find it astounding to see many adult passengers on trains indulging in cartoon books. Comic strips also appear in sports and tabloid papers.

Comic strips are not limited to popular entertainment; in fact, some textbooks for history and other subjects are written totally in comic strips. Readers span the social and intellectual spectrum. When students at the University of Tokyo—supposedly the best and brightest of that age group, and the future elite of the nation—began to publicly read *manga* at coffee shops near the campus in the 1970s, it was news. Now, manga may be the most sophisticated form of expression, according to some observers. Cartoons and comic strips have also become a major attraction in movie theaters and on television.

TEZUKA Osamu (1928–1989), the leading manga artist in postwar Japan, raised the manga to a serious art form, a medium through which to present complex characters and themes. Tezuka started to publish stories in cartoon strips in a boys' magazine in 1946 when he was a medical student. *Shin takarajima* (New Treasure Island, 1947) was his first hit. He created characters for his manga through innovative adaptation of characters in Walt Disney's animated films. He is said to have watched *Bambi* eighty times, memorizing every frame. Tezuka's best-known creation was *Tetsuwan Atomu* (Astro Boy), published in series from 1951 to 1969. This manga was a series of adventure stories about a robot boy, named Atom, in the twenty-first century. Atom had superhuman powers, such as the ability to fly in his jet-powered shoes, and a ten-thousand horsepower punch, which he used to fight for truth and justice. Tezuka began making animated cartoons in 1956. His Atom character was the star in Japan's first regularly scheduled TV cartoon show in 1963. In his later years Tezuka produced more complex stories, such as the life of Buddha and stories from the Old Testament.

Another postwar cartoon character with enduring popularity is Sazae-san, a creation of HASEGAWA Machiko (1920–1992). The four-frame cartoon strips humorously sketch the everyday life of Sazae-san, a young housewife. Hasegawa gave marine-related names to all the characters in her cartoons. Sazae's (a popular marine snail) Isono (seashore) family was an ordinary middle-class family who lived in an old urban neighborhood where children played together around the house. She lived with her husband, Masuo (trout); father, Namihei (flat wave); mother, Fune (boat); younger brother, Katsuo (bonito); younger sister, Wakame (a kind of sea plant); and her toddler daughter, Tara (cod). Both her father and husband are ordinary "salary men." Sazae and her mother stay home, and Tara plays with a neighborhood boy, Irura (caviar). The Sazae-san series first appeared in *Asahi Shimbun*, the most widely circulated newspaper, in 1949 and continued until 1974. It has been published in multivolume collected works as well.

Cartoonists have also functioned as social critics who express popular sentiment about political events and social conditions. The most prominent were YOKOYAMA Ryuichi, KONDO Hidezo, and SHIMIZU Kon; their cartoons were regularly featured in major newspapers and magazines during the postwar era. Shimizu's amorous images of *kappa*, a legendary amphibious creature with supernatural power, had fallible human feelings including a love of drinking *sake*.

Another outstanding cartoonist, MIZUKI Shigeru, specialized in ghosts and other supernatural phenomena in local folktales. Whereas children used to listen to ghost stories told by their grandparents, now they see the images of those creatures in cartoon books and animated TV cartoons.

FUJIKO Fujio, the joint artist name of FUJIMOTO Hiroshi and ABIKO Motoo, collaborated to create *Obake no Q-Taro* (Q-Taro the Ghost), an enormously popular TV cartoon in the 1960s. They subsequently created the even more successful *Doraemon*, which made its debut in educational magazines in 1969 and has been aired since 1979 as a TV cartoon. Doraemon is a personification of the cat friend of a 10-year-old schoolboy, Nobita. This striped cat, which has supernatural power to rescue Nobita in crises, is a time-traveling robot from the twenty-second century.

Nowadays, children get acquainted with cartoon characters on television screens. Many cartoon shows are aired every day on TV—there are fifty or more in the Tokyo area alone—and they compete with each other for audiences. Among the more successful cartoon series in recent years, IKEDA Riyoko's *Berusaiyu no bara* (The Rose of Versailles) centers on a beautiful young heroine.

The *anime* (animated film) is used as a medium for conveying messages on serious social and environmental issues by leading cartoon artists. MIYAZAKI Hayao (1941–) is the most well known. His 1984 film *Nausica of the Valley of the Wind* is an epic eco-fable about a young girl's struggle to survive in a poisoned world filled with warring tribes and insects. It won a series of prizes, including first prize at a science fiction festival in Paris, and had great box office success. In 1988, Miyazaki produced *Tonari no Totoro* (My Neighbor Totoro), the story of a fantasy creature in a paradisical countryside. In 1991 he produced *Omoide poroporo* (Only Yesterday), which is about a journey of self-discovery by a 27-year-old woman, an office worker in Tokyo.

NOTE

1. *Asahi shimbun Japan Almanac* (Tokyo: Asahi Shimbunsa, 1997), pp. 262–264.

11

Social Customs and Lifestyle

Earlier chapters have discussed manners and customs related to religious rituals, festivals, food, clothing, housing, marriage, and other aspects of Japanese life. This chapter elaborates on additional important features of social life in Japan. People are very mindful of sending the right kind of gifts and spend a lot of time and money on customary gifts. The *meishi* (business card) is used more extensively in Japan than in the United States. It is not just for business relations in Japan; it is a respectful manner by which to introduce oneself to others. The personal seal is another important element of social and business life in Japan, just as the personal signature is in the United States.

Gift-Giving

Many foreign observers have reported that Japanese tourists are busy shopping wherever they visit. Indeed, they do spend a lot of time shopping for gifts for their family and friends. It is a custom to bring some *omiyage* (souvenirs) from places they have visited and to share them with family and friends. In the old days when traveling long distance was very costly and even dangerous, people used to give travelers a parting gift of cash. This custom continued until the very recent past, when many Japanese began to travel abroad. Travelers who received a parting gift were naturally obliged to bring back souvenirs in return. Nowadays, special local products that would make good souvenirs are sold in department stores in every city in Japan. Even overseas souvenir goods are sold at airport gift shops so that travelers can order them before they start traveling.

There are certain common elements in gift-giving in many countries: people give gifts to children on their birthdays, graduation, and entrance to college; even wedding gifts and flowers (incense money in Japan) at funerals are universal. In addition to these, in Japan there are annual gift-giving seasons. Indeed, gifts are regarded as useful, although sometimes burdensome, in maintaining good social relations.

The art of sending appropriate gifts is important in social relations in Japan, and many guidebooks are published on it. A book written by a seasoned master of the tea ceremony includes advice related to gift-giving.[1] People are always searching for the most sensible way of giving gifts without falling into mannerisms. The standard expression in Japanese for "this is a small present for you" is *"kore wa tsumaranai mono desuga"* (this is not a worthwhile thing, but . . .).

There are two main gift-giving seasons in Japan: one at the end of the year (*seibo*), and the other in mid-year (*chugen*). Gifts sent out during these seasons are not as personal as those sent for Christmas or birthdays. The purpose of sending gifts at *seibo* and *chugen* is to express thanks to those who have been helpful in the past and/or those whose help is anticipated in the future; they indicate wishes for a long-lasting relationship. People send seasonal gifts to their supervisors at work to show respect. Married couples send them to those who served as the ritual go-betweens at their marriage. Some people send them to their family doctors. Parents send them to their children's teachers of calligraphy, music, or other lessons that take place at the teachers' homes. Moreover, gift-giving is not limited to individuals. Companies and business establishments send gifts to their patrons, partners, and loyal customers at the appropriate seasons. Neighborhood green grocers, cleaners, and other kinds of retailers and services also distribute small tokens of thanks to their customers. Such gifts are typically wall calendars for *seibo* and handheld fans for *chugen*, with store names and telephone numbers printed on them.

Individuals typically send preserved food or drink for seasonal gifts. Department stores and retail shops do a brisk business during the gift-giving seasons, taking orders for deliveries. In the old days, it was customary to pay a visit for greeting and delivering gifts during *seibo* and *chugen* seasons; however, in today's busy world people send most of their gifts through store delivery services and convey their greetings, if necessary, on postcards. Just as at New Years, Japanese people send greeting cards in mid-summer.

The timing of greetings and gifts is very important. Ideally, as one tea master says, the *seibo* gift should be delivered between December 10 and 20, and the *chugen* gift between July 1 and 15. If one misses these periods, the greeting words on the *noshigami* (formal cover sheet on the gift box) should be modified. For example, the word for New Years gift is more appropriate than the word for the *seibo* if the gift is to be delivered too close to the new year.

Appropriate gift items and the value of seasonal gifts vary according to the relationship between sender and recipient. Most gift sets advertised by department stores were priced between two thousand and twenty thousand yen in the 1990s (about $20 to $200, with between 100 and 130 yen per 1 U.S. dollar).

In many cases, recipients send return gifts. If the original gift was for a wedding, special birthday in advanced age, or completion of a new house, it is appropriate to send a return gift in the same amount as the original gift, if it was from one's inferiors (that is, a junior in social rank, which normally means less income). If it was from one's superiors or equals, the return gift should be about one-half the value of the original gift. Return gifts on joyous occasions are for the purpose of sharing the joy with those who gave the gifts.

Return gifts on sad occasions are supposed to be one-half or one-third the value of the original, regardless of the social relationship. Nowadays, many people donate the portion of "incense money" gifts at funerals to charities instead of sending out return gifts to individual gift givers. Still, the bereaved family sends out cards expressing thanks for the gifts and explaining to which organization the return money has been donated.

For some kinds of gifts, such as those for children, it is not necessary to send return gifts. Actually, gifts at *seibo* or *chugen* do not require return gifts, either. However, individuals and institutions normally send gifts to each other anyway.

Aside from annual gifts and those for special occasions, people customarily take a sweet or fruits when they visit other people at home. In the old days, when a family moved to a new neighborhood, the wife or husband would visit the neighboring families with a small gift such as a hand towel. This was a way to introduce themselves to the neighbors and establish friendly relations.

MEISHI (BUSINESS CARD)

The first thing a Japanese person does when introducing himself or herself is to present a *meishi* (business card). The other party reciprocates immediately. The card bears the name of the company or organization one belongs to, with specific information on the title one holds. The most properly printed meishi should have one's home address and telephone number in addition to the business address and number. However, meishi for purely business use do not require the home address. Meishi is now used for convenience in business relations. The protocols concerning meishi reflect an aspect of the hierarchical social relations in Japan. Everyone has to figure out how to treat each other in a manner appropriate to rank and status.

INKAN OR HANKO (PERSONAL SEAL)

Whereas Americans and Europeans use their signature on legal documents, the Japanese use a personal seal. Handwritten signatures are not recognized except in very special cases. Both individuals and organizations are supposed to have seals of their own. The seal of an individual normally has his or her surname only.

There are two categories of seals. *Jitsuin* (real seal) is used for formal legal documents, such as deeds, contracts, and wills. Individuals and organizations register their seals at the local government office.

Mitomein, sometimes called *sammonban*, is used for less formal documents such as passbook savings accounts at banks. When opening an account, the individual registers his or her seal at the bank and uses the same seal when withdrawing funds from the account. *Sammonban* (literally, "three penny seal") for common surnames are sold at stationery stores everywhere. Of course, false use of someone else's seal is a crime but is possible, just as forging a signature is possible. People are advised not to keep their seals together with their savings passbook. In Japan, personal checks are not used; instead people use cash or credit cards. For remittance of money, the post office and banks provide various services.

BOWING

The Japanese express respect, apology, and affection by bowing. There are methods of silent bowing and bowing with words of greeting. For various formal situations, such as expressing condolence and congratulations, there are standard phrases spoken while bowing.

The depth and duration of bowing vary depending on the situation and the relationship of the people involved. To bow while either standing or sitting on *tatami* floor, one bends the upper half of the body from the waist. When sitting on *tatami* floor, both hands touch the floor in front of one's knees. When bowing deep on the floor, both palms are put on the floor and the forehead almost touches the floor. To bow while standing, one keeps both hands straight on either side or folds them in front.

The manner of bowing is supposed to express one's personal style and personality. There is a proverb that says, "The richer the crop a rice plant grows, the deeper the ear bends." It expresses the idea that the more mature a person is, the more courteous the person becomes. A person who does not know how to lower the head is compared to an ear of rice that stands upright because it is empty.

People bow to express their thanks in more than an ordinary manner. Instead of just saying "Thank you," they bow when they mean to express sincere thanks. People also bow when begging or pleading. To express sincere apology, it is important to bow deeply. When a Japanese corporation announces its bankruptcy or acknowledges its responsibility in causing a social problem, the top officials apologize in public by deeply bowing toward assembled representatives of the public. Such scenes are often televised and published in newspapers.

When individuals are introduced to each other, they bow while exchanging *meisi* (business cards). When they part after conversation, they bow to each other to express good wishes. Hand-shaking has been adopted to a limited extent as a socially accepted form of greeting, but only among friends and people of equal social rank.

Bowing is the universal form of greeting in Japan. When saying "Hello," "Good morning," or "Good-bye," people bow to each other. Office workers on the first business day of the new year bow to their bosses and to each other, saying "Happy New Year," and thank each other for help during the past year. Bowing in television programs is very common. News reporters and program hosts bow to the viewers at the beginning and end of each show.

To express affection, even among family members, people bow. When a traditional wife sees off her husband leaving for work in the morning, she bows to him at the household gate. When the husband returns home, she comes to the entrance hall and is ready to greet him sitting on the floor by bowing with three center fingers of both hands on the floor. This extremely formal style is generally called "the Ogasawara style" after the name of the family of etiquette teachers. It was developed among upper-rank samurai families during the Tokugawa period and is known as the most elegant style of etiquette.

In Japan today, the extremely formal style of the feudal past has been discarded; however, alternatives for bowing have not developed. Hugging and kissing are not quite accepted as forms of greeting. People hug or kiss only their own babies and very young children. Hugging among family members takes place only in very extraordinary situations, such as in an airport lobby when hostages of a hijacked airplane are repatriated. In ordinary situations, young couples may hug each other when saying good-bye at the airport, but not members of the older generation. When I visit Japan once a year, my elderly mother bows to me when I arrive at home. When we say good-bye to each other at the end of my visit, we also bow. I do not hug her because she would be alarmed if I did. Hugging is simply not an accepted form of greeting among grown-up family members.

In Japan, bowing is the most natural expression of respect for others. It is also an indication of social distance between individuals. Because the manner of bowing is an expression of a complex code of behavior, very often bowing while greeting lasts for a considerable time. To foreigners the individuals may appear to be bobbing their heads up and down meaninglessly; however, they are actually following a mutually understood pattern and rhythm. Foreigners who are not familiar with the subtlety of these protocols should not mimic Japanese-style bowing superficially. Manners of expressing one's feelings may be different from one society to another, but genuine feelings conveyed in a reserved manner can cut across cultural boundaries.

NOTE

1. Yaeko Shiozaki, *Saho jiten* (The Illustrated Encyclopedia of Manners) (Tokyo: Shogakukan, 1996).

Glossary

anime   animated film

apato   apartment

aragoto   "rough business" type of *kabuki* acting

asagohan, asameshi   breakfast

aware   sorrow; gentle melancholy

bakufu   "government from the military tent"; shogunate

bangohan   supper

banka   eulogy

benshi   narrator for a silent movie

bento   box lunch

biwa   Japanese lute with four strings

bon odori   folk dance at Mid-Summer festival

bonsai   art of growing miniature trees in containers; potted dwarf trees

bugaku   ancient Japanese court dance and music

bunraku   puppet theater

burakumin   "people of the hamlet," a euphemistic term for outcasts

bushi (samurai)   warrior

butsudan   ancestral altar (Buddhist)

chakaiseki ryori   meal served at a tea ceremony

chanoma   family room for dining and sitting in a Japanese house

chanoyu   "hot water for tea"; tea ceremony

chashitsu   room for a tea ceremony

chigai-dana   decorative shelf in an alcove

choka   long poem

daijosai   "great feast ceremony" of enthronement

daiku   carpenter

daimyo   regional feudal lord

danchi   apartment housing project developed by Japan Housing Corporation

DK   "dining kitchen" of an apartment house

dogu   earthen figurines of prehistoric age

domburi   large rice bowl, or rice covered with cooked food served in it

Edokko   multi-generational residents of old downtown section of Tokyo (formerly Edo)

ema   "picture horse" votive plaque dedicated to Shinto shrine

emakimono   picture scroll

engawa   long, narrow veranda made of unfinished wood planks

enka   a type of popular song in vogue in the 1950s

fue   flute

funa-asobi   outing on a pleasure boat

fusuma   wood-framed sliding door covered with thick paper

futon   mattress or comforter filled with cotton or synthetic fiber

gagaku   "elegant music"; ritual music ensemble of the imperial court

garan   a layout pattern of the Buddhist temple compound

geisha   courtesans and entertainers at banquets at Japanese-style restaurants

geta   wooden stilted sandals with thongs

gidayu-bushi   "Gidayu-tune"; a school of chanting for puppet theater

gohan   cooked rice; meal

haiku   short (17-syllable) poetry form

hakama   wide trousers or skirt to wear over *kimono*

hanamichi   "flower path"; extension from the stage to the back of the kabuki theater

haniwa   clay cylinder and terra-cotta figurine of the Kofun (tomb) period

hanko   personal seal

haori   half-length over-kimono

happi   cotton jacket with stencil-dyed family crest or shop name

hashi   chopsticks

hashigakari   passageway for the noh stage

hassun   appetizer dish

hatsumono   the earliest shipment of fish or vegetable of the season

hayagawari   quick change of an actor's costume on the stage

hinomaru bento   "rising sun lunchbox"; lunch consisting of rice in a rectangular lunchbox and a pickled plum in its center

hiru gohan   "noon meal"; lunch

hogaku   Japanese traditional music

honmaru   the central enclosure of a castle

honzen ryori   the most formal banquet food

hotoke   Buddha

ie   family

iemoto   the head family of a school of art who transmits the authentic teaching of the school

ihai   spirit tablet

ikebana   flower arrangement

iki   "smart" or "cool"

inari   deity of fox spirit

inkan   personal seal

jidai-geki   period drama

jidai-mono   historical piece of performing art

jiki   porcelain

jitsuin   "real seal"; an officially registered seal

jiutai   chorus of performing theater

jodo   "pure land"; Buddhist paradise

joruri   narrative chanting accompanied by *shamisen* at performing theater

jubako   a set of lacquer boxes for food that are stacked on top of each other

kabuki   theatrical performance popular among townsmen during the Tokugawa period

kado   "the way of flower"; flower arrangement

kadomatsu   pine branch decoration at household gate for New Years

kaiseki ryori   general banquet food, traditional Japanese style

kaiyu   many-pleasure

kakizome   the first exercise of brush writing of the New Year

kami   superior being; Shinto deity

kamidana   altar of a Shinto deity

kamigata   cultural center in Kansai area

kami-kaze   "divine wind"

kamite   upper (left) side of the stage of *kabuki* theater

kana   two sets of Japanese syllabary systems, namely, katakana and hiragana

kanji   Chinese characters

kanshi   Chinese poem

kansho   contemplation

karaoke   "empty orchestra"; accompaniment orchestra without song

kare-sansui   "dry mountain stream" (a form of landscape garden)

kata   forms or patterns of stylized gesture in theatrical performance

katsudo shashin   motion picture

katsuobushi   dried bonito fillet

katsura-mono   wig play of *noh* drama

kayokyoku   popular songs in vogue in early twentieth-century Japan

kegare   defilement; pollution

kimono   traditional Japanese clothes

kodan   storytelling or recitation for popular entertainment

kogei   handicraft art

kojin   stove god

koken   stage assistant

koku   the unit of measurement of grain (about five bushels)

kondo   (literally, golden hall) the main hall of a Buddhist temple

koseki   household register

koshimaki   wrap-around underskirt for *kimono*

kotatsu   foot warmer with source of heat under a wooden framework covered with quilting

koto   a six foot-long zither with thirteen strings

kozutsumi   small hand drum

kurogo   stage assistant in black costume

kyogen   short farce played between *noh* dramas

makunouchi bento   full-course box lunch

manga   comics; cartoons

manshon   "mansion"; condominium

manzai   comic banter performed by two artists

maritsuki   bouncing balls

matsuri   festival

matsuri bayashi   music ensemble at a festival

meishi   business card

meshi   cooked rice; meal

miai   formal interview for marriage arrangement

mie   intensely posed gesture in *kabuki* performance

minyo   local folk song

miso   bean paste

mitome-in   personal seal for everyday use

miya-daiku   shrine carpenter

monogatari   tale

mono-no-aware   "sadness of things"

montsuki   formal *kimono* with family crest stencil-dyed or embroidered on it

moribana   "piled-up flowers"; a form of flower arrangement

muko-zuke   side dish

nagajuban   under-kimono

nagauta   "long music"; narrative music of *kabuki* theater

nagaya   wood-frame, one-story row house

nageire   "thrown-in flowers"; a form of flower arrangement

nakoodo   go-between for marriage arrangement

natto   fermented soy beans

nengajo   New Years greeting card

niboshi   dried baby sardines

Nihonto   Japanese sword

nijiriguchi   crawling-in entrance to a tea ceremony room

ningen kokuho   "living national treasure"; a person who is designated by the government as the holder of an important cultural property, such as talent and skill in performing or handicraft art

ningyo joruri   puppet theater

ninomaru   the second enclosure of a castle

noborigama   climbing kiln

noh   a classic form of drama with music and masked dance

noh-men   *noh* mask

norito   chanting of prayer in Shinto ritual

noshigami   formal cover sheet on gift box

nukazuke   vegetable pickled in fermented rice bran

o-   "honorable" or "respectfully presented" (a prefix)

obi   sash for *kimono*

o-chazuke   a bowl of rice served with hot green tea to pour over it

o-chugen   mid-summer gift

okazu   side dish of steamed rice

o-mikoshi   portable Shinto shrine

o-mikuji   "honorable sacred lot"; oracle slips of Shinto shrine

o-miyage   "respectfully presented souvenir"

onnagata   a male actor who plays a female role in *kabuki* theater

osechi ryori   New Years feast

o-seibo   end-of-the-year gift

oshiire   closet

o-tedama   juggling balls made of cloth with dried beans in them

ozutsumi   large hand drum

pachinko   vertical pinball game

rakugo   comic monologue with punch lines at the end for popular entertainment

renga   linked verses

rikka   standing or vertical-style flower arrangement

ronin   masterless *samurai*

ryotei   high-class restaurants of Japanese-style cuisine

sabi   restrained beauty

sake   rice wine

samurai (bushi)   "man in waiting"; medieval warrior

sankin kotai   "alternate attendance"

sanmonban   "three penny seal"; ready-made personal seals on sale in stationery stores

sannomaru   the third enclosure of a castle

sashimi   sliced raw fish

seika (shoka)   a form of flower arrangement

senryu   satiric short poem

senshoku   dyeing and weaving

seto-mono   "seto ware"; porcelain for everyday use

sewa-mono   *kabuki* drama about contemporary society or family life

shakuhachi   vertical flute made of bamboo near its root

shamisen (samisen)   three-stringed plucked lute

shi   poem

shikki   lacquer ware

shimenawa   straw rope to mark the sacred place at a Shinto shrine; also used as New Years decoration of a house

shimote   lower (right) side of the stage

shinden-zukuri   *shinden* ("main hall")-centered mansion

shite   the primary actor of *noh* drama

shiwasu   the last month of a year

shochu mimai   mid-summer greetings

shodo   calligraphy

shogi   Japanese chess

shogun (seii taishogun)   "great general who quells barbarians"; the head of a government by warriors

shoheiga   paintings on screens and sliding doors

shoin   studio

shoin-zukuri   "studio style" or "study-alcove style" residential architecture

shoji   wood-framed sliding door with lattice covered with translucent paper

shosa-goto   action-centered piece of *kabuki* performance

shoyu   soy sauce

shun   prime time of vegetable or fish of the season

shushoku   staple food

shuyu   stroll

soba   buckwheat; buckwheat noodle

somon   poems exchanged between two individuals

sukiya-zukuri   *sukiya* (variations of tea ceremony room)-style residential architecture

supar   supermarket

sushi   rice seasoned with vinegar and arranged with seafood or vegetable

tabi   socks with slit between big toe and the other toes

taiko   large drum

tanka   "short poem" with 31 syllables

tatami   straw mat covered with woven surface

tate   act of stylized fighting on *kabuki* stage

tenshukaku   donjon or the main tower complex of a castle

toki   ceramic ware

toko-bashira   the main pillar of *tokonoma* alcove

tokonoma   decorative alcove in a formal parlor

torii   sacred arch at the entrance of a Shinto shrine

tsuke   sound effect of wooden clappers struck against the floor to enhance actions on *kabuki* stage

tsukuri-mono   props on stage of performing art

tsumi   sin

tsuno-kakushi   "horn cover"; headgear of a new bride

tsure   a companion of the primary or secondary actor of *noh* drama

uji   tribal unit in prehistoric age

ujigami   "deity of uji"; local ancestral deity

ukiyo   "sorrowful world" or "floating world"

unagi eel

urushi lacquer made of sap of urushi tree

utai chanting of prose in the style of *noh* drama

wabi forlornness

wafuku Japanese-style clothes

waka Japanese poem

waki the secondary actor of *noh* drama

wasabi horseradish

yabo rustic; unfashionable; overly serious

yamato-e Japanese-style painting

yofuku Western-style clothes

yugen subtle profundity

yukata stencil-dyed cotton *kimono*

zabuton flat, square cushion

zaibatsu "financial clique"; big business conglomerate

zashiki formal parlor covered with *tatami* mats

zori platform sandals with thongs

Suggested Readings

GENERAL INFORMATION

Aoki, Michiko Y., and Margaret B. Dardess, comps. *As the Japanese See It: Past and Present*. Honolulu: University Press of Hawaii, 1981.

Colcutt, Martin, Marius Jansen, and Isao Kumakura. *Cultural Atlas of Japan*. New York: Facts on Life Publication, 1988.

Domeki, Kyozaburo, and Kenji, Iwamoto. *Japanese Culture*, About Japan series, No. 11. Tokyo: Foreign Press Center, 1979, 1993.

Hall, John, and Richard K. Beardslay, eds. *Twelve Doors to Japan*. New York: McGraw-Hill, 1965.

Hendry, Joy. *Understanding Japanese Society*. London and New York: Routledge, 1989.

An Illustrated Encyclopedia. Tokyo: Kodansha International, 1993.

Japan As It Is: A Bilingual Guide, rev. ed. Tokyo: Gakken, 1990.

Japan: Profile of a Nation. Tokyo: Kodansha International, 1994.

Kodansha Encyclopedia of Japan. Tokyo: Kodansha International, 1983. Eight volumes plus index volume and 1986 Supplement.

Nippon Steel Human Resources Development Co., Ltd. *Nippon: The Land and Its People*. Tokyo: Gakuseisha, 1988.

Pyle, Kenneth B. *The Making of Modern Japan*. Lexington, MA: D. C. Heath and Co., 1996.

Reischauer, Edwin O. *Japan: The Story of a Nation*, 3rd ed. New York: Alfred A. Knopf, 1981.

Reischauer, Edwin O., and Marius B. Jansen. *The Japanese Today, Change and Continuity*. Cambridge, MA: Harvard University Press, 1995.

Tiedemann, Arthur E. *An Introduction to Japanese Civilization*. New York: Columbia University Press, 1974.

Totman, Conrad. *Japan before Perry: A Short History*. Berkeley: University of California Press, 1981.

THOUGHT AND RELIGION

Benedict, Ruth. *The Chrysanthemum and the Sword: Patterns of Japanese Culture*. Boston: Houghton Mifflin, 1946.

Doi, Takeo. *The Anatomy of Dependence*. Tokyo: Kodansha International, 1973.

Earhart, Byron H. *Japanese Religion: Unity and Diversity*. Belmont, CA: Dickenson Publishing, 1974.

Hardacre, Helen. *Shinto and the State, 1868–1988*. Princeton, NJ: Princeton University Press, 1991.

Tsunoda, Ryusaku, Theodore De Bary, and Donald Keene, eds. *Sources of Japanese Tradition*. New York: Columbia University Press, 1958.

LANGUAGE AND LITERATURE

Habein, Yaeko Sato. *The History of the Japanese Written Language*. Tokyo: University of Tokyo Press (distributed by Columbia University Press), 1984.

Kato, Shuichi. *A History of Japanese Literature*, 3 vols. Tokyo: Kodansha International, 1979, 1981.

Keene, Donald. *Japanese Literature: An Introduction for Western Readers*. New York: Grove Press, 1955.

———, comp. and ed. *Anthology of Japanese Literature: From the Earliest Era to the Mid-Nineteenth Century*. New York: Grove Press, 1955.

Miller, Roy Andrew. *Origins of the Japanese Language*. Seattle: University of Washington Press, 1980.

Ueda, Makoto, ed. and trans. *Modern Japanese Tanka: An Anthology*. New York: Columbia University Press, 1996.

ARTS AND ARCHITECTURE

A Guide to Japanese Architecture. Tokyo: Shinkenchikusha, 1973.

Ito, Nobuo. "Buddhist Architecture." and "Castles," In *Kodansha Encyclopedia of Japan*, Tokyo: Kodansha International, 1983, vol. 1.

Ito, Nobuo. "Shinto Architecture." In *Kodansha Encyclopedia of Japan*. Tokyo: Kodansha International, 1983, vol. 7.

Kiritani, Elizabeth. *Vanishing Japan: Traditions, Crafts, and Culture*. Rutland, VT: Charles E. Tuttle, 1995.

Paine, Robert Treat, and Alexander Soper. *The Art and Architecture of Japan*. Baltimore, Md.: Penguin Books, 1955. 3rd ed./with revision by D. B. Waterhouse Harmondworth, Middlesex, Penguin, 1981.

Seike, Kiyosi. "Architecture, Modern," and "Architecture, Traditional Domestic." In *Kodansha Encyclopedia of Japan*, Tokyo: Kodansha International, 1983, vol. 1.

Varley, Paul. *Japanese Culture: A Short History*. New York: Praeger, 1973.

Varley, Paul, and Isao Kumakura, eds. *Tea in Japan: Essays on the History of Chanoyu*. Honolulu: University of Hawaii Press, 1989.

CUISINE

Tsuji, Shizuo. "Cooking, Japanese." In *Kodansha Encyclopedia of Japan*, Tokyo: Kodansha International, 1983, vol. 2.

WOMEN AND FAMILY LIFE

Bando, Sugahara Mariko. *Japanese Women Yesterday and Today*. Tokyo: Foreign Press Center, 1996.

Bernstein, Gail Lee, ed. *Recreating Japanese Women, 1600–1945*. Berkeley: University of California Press, 1991.

Brinton, Mary C. *Women and the Economic Miracle*. Berkeley: University of California Press, 1994.

Edwards, Walter. *Modern Japan through Its Weddings: Gender, Person, and Society in Ritual Portrayal*. Stanford, CA: Stanford University Press, 1989.

Iwao, Sumiko. *The Japanese Women: Traditional Image and Changing Reality*. New York: Free Press, 1993; Cambridge, MA: Harvard University Press, 1994.

Plath, D. W. *Long Engagements: Maturity in Modern Japan*. Stanford, CA: Stanford University Press, 1980.

Smith, Robert J., and Ella Lury Wiswell. *The Women of Sue Mura*. Chicago: University of Chicago Press, 1984.

Vogel, Ezra. *Japan's New Middle Class: The Salary Man and His Family in a Tokyo Suburb*, 2nd ed. with a new chapter by Suzanne Hall Vogel, "Beyond Success—Mamachi Thirty Years Later." Berkeley: University of California Press, 1991.

Yuzawa, Yasuhiko. *Japanese Families*. Tokyo: Foreign Press Center, 1994.

CLOTHING

Terai, Minako, and Setsuko Otsuka. "Kimono." In *Kodansha Encyclopedia of Japan*, Tokyo: Kodansha International, 1983, vol. 4.

Leisure and Entertainment

Anderson, J. L. "Film, Japanese." In *Kodansha Encyclopedia of Japan*, Tokyo: Kodansha International, 1983, vol. 2.

Richie, Donald. *Japanese Cinema: An Introduction*. Hong Kong: Oxford University Press, 1990.

Shilling, Mark. *The Encyclopedia of Japanese Popular Culture*. New York: Weatherhill, 1997.

Index

About the Author

NORIKO KAMACHI is Professor of history at the University of Michigan, Dearborn. She is the author of *Reform in China* (1981) and *Japanese Studies of Modern China since 1953* (1975).